EVERYDAY INDIAN

EVERYDAY INDIAN

100 FAST, FRESH, AND HEALTHY RECIPES

BAL ARNESON

whitecap

Whitecap Books is known for its expertise in the cookbook market, and has produced some of the most innovative and familiar titles found in kitchens across North America. Visit our website at www.whitecap.ca.

Edited by Elaine Jones
Proofread by Melva McLean
Design by Mauve Pagé
Food photography by Tracey Kusiewicz
Food styling by Bal Arneson and Tracey Kusiewicz
Additional photography by Michelle Mayne, except for pages ii, 7, and 183 (left) by Tracey Kusiewicz, page 72 by Igor Badalassi, page 102 by Andrea Kratzenberg, and page 138 by Ibon San Martin

Printed in China

The publisher would like to thank the following generous sponsors of this project:

- Denby
- Capers Whole Foods
- Oneida

Library and Archives Canada Cataloguing in Publication

Arneson, Bal, 1972–
Everyday Indian : 100 fast, fresh, and healthy recipes / Bal Arneson.

Includes index.
ISBN 978-1-55285-948-3

1. Cookery, Indic. I. Title.

TX724.5.I4A74 2009 641.5954 C2008-905590-X

The publisher acknowledges the financial support of the Government of Canada through the Book Publishing Industry Development Program (BPIDP) and the Province of British Columbia through the Book Publishing Tax Credit.

09 10 11 12 13 5 4 3 2

FOR MY DAUGHTER, ANOOP, AND SON, AARON,
WHO INSPIRE ME TO MAKE HEALTHY MEALS

AND FOR BRAD, WHO ALWAYS
PROVIDES UNCONDITIONAL SUPPORT

contents

introduction

HEALTHY FOOD, HEALTHY MIND, AND HEALTHY BODY

The recipes in this book reflect my love of creating simple and wholesome, fresh and fast Indian food without compromising flavour. These recipes are made with basic, everyday, easily accessible ingredients. I have simplified the cooking steps so no special cooking ability is required to make an authentic, gourmet Indian meal in less time than it would take to go out to eat.

I called this book *Everyday Indian* because you shouldn't have to go to a restaurant to enjoy the great flavours of Indian food, nor should you view an Indian meal as an occasional treat. And eating well doesn't mean we need to spend hours each day in the kitchen. With a little practice, you can take any recipe in this book, any day of the week, and create a delicious, healthy dish in 20 to 25 minutes.

I also believe we need to make conscious decisions about what goes into our bodies. There are many environmental factors we cannot control, but we can control what we eat. Farmers' markets offer plentiful local produce, and it is very encouraging to see that organic food is now available in supermarkets at reasonable prices. Making a few small changes, such as using whole grains, whole wheat flour, brown rice, and low-fat yogurt (in place of cream), can make a great difference to our overall well-being. Every day I receive emails from people telling me that after trying my recipes they don't feel bloated the next day, unlike when they make other recipes or eat at Indian restaurants.

While I have come a long way from the village in Punjab, northern India, where I was raised, my cooking style and philosophy of food are rooted there.

I learned to cook at a young age; I had no choice when it came to doing household chores, including cooking. Girls were expected to know how to cook various dishes and be able to prepare large amounts to feed the extended family. Most women were responsible for household chores, and men worked outside the home.

My mother and all the other women in the village could never spend long hours in the kitchen. They had to do all their other chores by hand, without any electric appliances such as dishwashers, washers and dryers, and vacuum cleaners, and water had to be fetched from the hand pump shared by several families. Fuel was scarce, so cooking time had to be quick (with the exception of beans, chickpeas, and lentils, which could be left to cook over the coals in the barbecue pit), and most dishes took no more than 20 minutes. For each meal, we started the clay barbecue pit from scratch by adding dried cow dung and sticks.

My earliest memories of food include overhearing the conversations of my female cousins: "You must know how to make perfect round rotis in order to please your husband and his family." One of our tasks was to make cow dung patties for fuel and so I practised making round rotis with the cow dung. When, at the age of nine, I was responsible for making rotis for the family, I picked only the perfectly round rotis for my father so that he would know I had mastered the task. Soon after, I was responsible for cooking the majority of our dinners.

From the beginning, I loved cooking because the kitchen gave me an opportunity to express my creativity and also the freedom that I did not have. Like most girls in my village, I had little or no independence. My whole life was planned for me by my elders: what I would wear, my hairstyle, the education I was allowed to have, and my future husband and in-laws.

At that time, girls in my village were educated not so they could become independent, but to add education to their résumé so that a suitable husband could be found. Since education was not the first priority, many girls left school after the tenth grade. I was the first generation and the first woman from my father's side of the family to graduate from high school, win a scholarship, and go on to college. As soon as I graduated from high school, my father started looking for a husband for me, but by that time the expectations had started changing a little. If the suitable partner lived overseas, a college education was encouraged and accepted for women. And so it was that I came to Canada via an arranged marriage at the age of 20, and a new chapter opened in my life.

When I first arrived I was scared and worried. Not only did I have to leave all my friends and family behind in the village, but I also had to live with absolute strangers—my in-laws. It took me a long time just to get over the shock of being able to have either hot or cold water simply by turning a tap. I didn't know the language or much about the culture of this new country, but what I loved from the beginning was that I was part of a multicultural community where I was able to access and experience all kinds of food from all over the world. I soon realized this was my new, global village.

I still remember my very first visit to a grocer; I thought I had died and gone to heaven when I saw the amount of food from every season and many different countries. What fascinated me most was a row containing hundreds of spices from all over the world. I had never imagined I would have the privilege of exploring all those spices in my cooking.

Over the following years, and through many important life changes, I continued my adventures in cooking, but now with all the modern conveniences! As a child I had sometimes stepped outside the rigid boundaries set for me by village life, but little did I know that my passion for cooking and creating recipes would lead to a new life and a successful career on the other side of the world. It would even give me the opportunity to participate in various fund-raising events that support women, children, and underprivileged families in our communities. Through it all, the important lessons learned in my mother's kitchen stuck with me: use fresh, organic ingredients and make it simple.

My husband, Brad, grew up in Trail, B.C., and he had never had Indian food before he met me. He often took leftover food to work for lunch, and my home-cooked Indian food became a popular topic of conversation in the lunchroom. The feedback I got was that people had never heard the words *healthy*, *quick*, and *Indian food* together before. I was also surprised and disappointed to find that the food in Indian restaurants was floating in cream and butter (my mother and other women in the village never used butter, relying on a few spices and seasonal fresh herbs and vegetables for flavour). When his co-workers asked Brad if I could teach them how to cook yummy Indian meals, it was the beginning of my cooking business.

Not only did the business help pay my tuition for my education degree from the University of British Columbia, but it also gave me a passion for sharing my recipes. Since then I have given hundreds of cooking classes all over British Columbia and in Calgary, Alberta. I love passing on cooking tips and telling stories about village life. The thing I like best, though, is that both men and women of different nationalities, including the new generation of Indo-Canadians, come to learn from me.

Though I have taught and fed hundreds of people, my most supportive critics are my 14-year-old daughter, Anoop, and four-year-old son, Aaron. They love Indian food and love cooking with me, but I make sure both learn the importance of healthy food and that the activity of cooking is not only for girls. I try my best to have a family cooking day at least once a week. Making rotis is one of the activities we all thoroughly enjoy. When Brad, Anoop, and Aaron roll their rotis, it is quite a sight. After ten years, Brad is still working on making his rotis thin and round. Anoop's always end up looking like Valentine cookies, and Aaron's look like spiders.

My sold-out cooking classes, along with my TV appearances and a story about my cooking in a local newspaper, generated hundreds of emails from people asking if I had a book. At that point I knew I had to write this cookbook because there was a huge demand for my approach to cooking, an approach that fits so well with today's busy, health-conscious lifestyle. I hope when you use this book, you will become as passionate as I am about cooking healthy, tasty, fast Indian food. Enjoy!

MY MASALA CABINET

It is a common misconception that Indian food is too complicated to make. Let me assure you that not only can Indian food be delicious, it can also be healthy and quick to prepare. At my cooking classes, people tell me what spices they have in their kitchen. Then I tell them that the only two spices I saw my mother use in her cooking were garam masala and ground turmeric, and these are still the only ones I use for everyday Indian cooking. They are sitting on my first shelf along with salt and pepper.

Having said that, there are a few more spices to experiment with, especially if you want to make garam masala from scratch. It's a good idea to start playing with one spice at a time to see what flavours you might enjoy. We all have different palates, and we must use them to guide our cooking.

The spices for the recipes in this book can be found in most grocery stores, health food stores, and ethnic markets. Most grocery stores or health food stores also carry flaxseed and grapeseed oils. The fresh ingredients you should always have on hand are onions, garlic, and ginger.

Overall, remember that cooking is a fun experience that can be enjoyed by the whole family. So pour yourself a glass of wine, get out your spices, and let's begin!

The Spices

Asafoetida, called *hing* in Punjabi, is a pale yellow powder that's used in savoury dishes. It has a very unpleasant smell when raw, but when cooked in hot oil, it adds a wonderful onion-like aroma to the food. It can also be purchased as a small, hardened lump, but because of its strong flavour it needs to be chopped in very small pieces before it is used.

Bay leaves are available in the spice aisle of any supermarket.

Cardamom comes in black, brown, and green pods. Usually all three are used to make chai tea. I have used green cardamom seeds in a few of my recipes. Most of the flavour is in the seeds, but you can grind the pods and seeds together. I use a coffee grinder.

Chana masala is similar to garam masala but contains mango powder and dried pomegranate seeds. It can be purchased in a small package from any supermarket, or you can make your own (see page 14).

Chat masala is a dried spice mixture contains several different spices, but the combination of mango powder, mint leaves, and asafoetida gives chat masala a very unique sweet and sour flavour. It can be purchased at local supermarkets or ethnic stores, or you can make your own (see page 13).

Cinnamon comes in bark (stick) or powdered form and is available everywhere. I use cinnamon sticks to make garam masala.

Coriander seeds are larger than peppercorns. I use them whole and in powder form. Coriander is an ingredient in garam masala, which is how it is used in most Punjabi cooking. It imparts a fine aroma and earthy flavours to food.

Cumin seeds have a nutty flavour. Sometimes I use ground cumin as well.

Curry leaves can be purchased fresh or frozen but they're not always available, so for all my recipes I have specified dried curry leaves. They still have great flavour, but fresh is always better, if you can find it. Look for it in ethnic markets.

Fennel seeds, known as *saunf* in northern India, are sometimes chewed after a meal as a digestive and breath freshener. Fennel seeds are long, rounded, and pale green and are very aromatic.

Fenugreek is called *methi* in Punjabi. Seeds as well as dried leaves are used for cooking; both are readily available in supermarkets.

Garam masala is a mixture of dried spices typically used in the northern part of India. This is available as a prepared mix, or you can make your own (see page 12).

Mango powder can be purchased in the ethnic aisles of supermarkets or ethnic stores.

Mustard seeds are small and round, and they can be yellow, brown or black. When toasted in hot oil, they give a nutty flavour to the food.

Peppercorns are available in white and black. Black peppercorns have more aroma and flavour. They are used in ground form to give heat to the food.

Pomegranate seeds are sun-dried and sold as *anardana*. You can find them in ethnic markets as whole seeds or in powdered form.

Sambar powder is a mix of strong flavourings, including asafoetida and dried curry leaves. It's available pre-made, or you can make your own (see page 17).

Spanish paprika, called *degi mirch* in Punjabi, is ground sweet red peppers. When I purchase it in Indian markets, the package is labelled Spanish paprika, with the Punjabi name written underneath.

Tamarind, or *imli* in Punjabi, is sold as a small block that contains seeds, flavourful flesh, and fibre. To use it, cut a smaller chunk (about a tablespoon) from the block and put it in a small bowl with enough hot water to cover it. Let it sit for 10 minutes. Use a fork to separate the seeds and the pulp. Strain the water though a small sieve. Discard the pulp and seeds and use the water.

Turmeric is a root that's related to ginger; ground turmeric gives a bright yellow colour to food.

health benefits of indian cooking

In the village where I grew up, we ate seasonal, organic food, and in all my cooking today I keep these health benefits in mind.

I always use grapeseed oil, not cream or ghee (clarified butter), for cooking, and I use flaxseed oil to moisten rotis and for salad dressings. Turmeric, either fresh or as a powder, is also something I like my children to eat on a regular basis, and I try my best to include garlic and ginger in the cooking. Here is some information on the ingredients I use every day.

Turmeric fights free radicals, protects the liver against toxins, aids circulation, lowers cholesterol levels, improves blood vessel health, and has antibiotic and anti-inflammatory properties. Once I broke my ankle while climbing a mango tree and my mother gave me warm milk with ground turmeric in it. It tasted horrible but helped me heal. This was a very common natural remedy for external and internal injuries.

Ginger fights inflammation, cleanses the colon, stimulates circulation, acts as a strong antioxidant, protects the liver and stomach, is useful for circulatory problems, and helps reduce fever, headache, nausea, and hot flashes.

Garlic detoxifies the body and protects against infection by enhancing the immune function, lowers blood pressure, improves circulation, and helps prevent colds, the flu, digestive problems, sinusitis, and yeast infections.

Flaxseed oil contains omega-3 essential fatty acids, is a great source of B vitamins, protein, and zinc, is low in saturated fats and calories, and contains no cholesterol. It promotes strong bones, nails, and teeth, and healthy skin.

Grapeseed oil is low in saturated fats, contains no cholesterol or sodium, and can be heated to temperatures as high as 485°F without producing dangerous and possibly carcinogenic free radicals. If possible, buy cold-pressed oil with no preservatives.

(This information is from *Prescription for Nutritional Healing*, 3rd edition, by Phyllis A. Balch, CNC.)

essential spices

Veronica

In India my mother would put all the garam masala ingredients on a large serving platter and leave them out in the hot sun to toast. We didn't have a food processor—no one in the village had any electric kitchen appliances—so a large stone bowl and a wide wooden stick were used to grind the spices. My mother would cover her face so the spices wouldn't go up her nose while she pounded them for a good half an hour until the masala was the consistency of a fine powder. I've included this recipe so you can choose to make your own, but I have also used store-bought garam masala, and the result is almost as satisfactory.

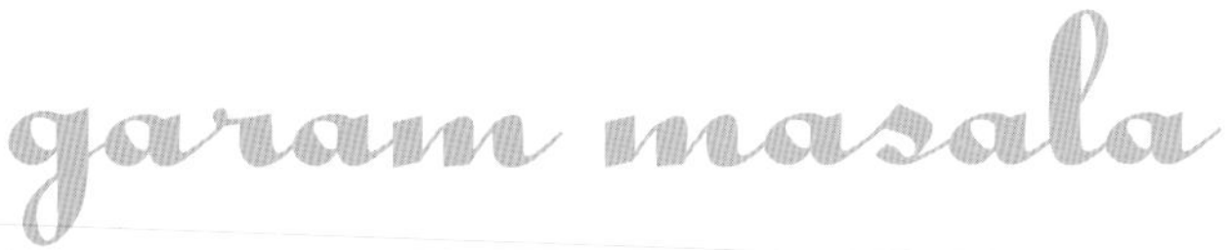

½ cup coriander seeds
½ cup cumin seeds
¼ cup dried curry leaves
¼ cup black peppercorns
3 whole cloves
2 black cardamom pods
2 cinnamon sticks, each 3 inches long
2 bay leaves

Preheat the oven to 325°F. Combine all the ingredients, spread them on a rimmed baking sheet, and toast in the oven for 15 minutes. Let cool and process to a fine powder in a grinder, such as a coffee grinder reserved for this purpose. Store in an airtight container in a cool place, for up to 3 months.

MAKES 1½ CUPS

Many people prefer this recipe to store-bought chat masala because it has a mild flavour. However, if you prefer something spicier and more heavy, use a packaged chat masala, which can be easily purchased from ethnic grocery stores.

chat masala

- 1 Tbsp mango powder
- 1 Tbsp ground cumin
- 1 Tbsp ground coriander
- 1 tsp pomegranate powder
- ¼ tsp ground dried ginger
- ¼ tsp salt
- ¼ tsp pepper

Combine all the ingredients in a bowl and mix well. Store in an airtight container in a cool place for up to 3 months.

NOTE For more of an enhanced flavour add 1 tsp fennel seeds and ¼ tsp mint powder.

MAKES ¼ CUP

*My dear friend Parminder's brother, Gopal bhaji (***bhaji** *means "brother"), owned a small restaurant in front of Parminder's house. Since I was a female I was not allowed to visit my friends' homes. However, I sneaked in a visit here and there, and every time I visited her house, Gopal bhaji made us a chickpea dish. He always used chana masala, which includes dried mango and pomegranate seed powder.*

chana masala

- 3 Tbsp ground coriander
- 3 Tbsp ground cumin
- 1 tsp mango powder
- 1 tsp pomegranate powder
- 1 tsp ground turmeric
- 1 tsp fenugreek leaves, crumbled
- ½ tsp red chili powder
- ½ tsp ground dried ginger
- ½ tsp garlic powder
- ½ tsp ground cardamom
- ½ tsp salt

Combine all the ingredients and mix well. Store in an airtight container in a cool place for up to 3 months.

NOTE As much as I love making my own masala, on many occasions I have purchased a package of chana masala from an Indian grocery store. You could also enhance the flavour by adding additional ingredients, such as whole cumin seeds and fresh garlic, when you're cooking.

MAKES ABOUT ½ CUP

I've noticed that most people who love Indian flavours also love Thai food. Both countries not only use similar spices but also use them in similar ways. For this recipe, I like to toast the spices in the oven first and then mix all the ingredients together. I haven't found a Thai restaurant with a healthy, low-fat menu; until then I'll keep cooking my fusion Thai food!

fusion curry paste

Step 1

- 1 tsp coriander seeds
- 1 tsp cumin seeds
- 1 tsp black peppercorns
- 1 dried red chili pepper
- 2 cardamom pods

Preheat the oven to 300°F. Combine all the ingredients on a rimmed baking sheet and toast for 15 minutes. Let cool and process to a fine powder in a small grinder, such as a coffee grinder reserved for this purpose.

Step 2

- ½ cup fresh cilantro
- 2 Tbsp finely chopped lemon grass
- 1 Tbsp grated ginger
- 1 Tbsp grated garlic
- 1 Tbsp lime juice
- 1 tsp lime zest
- 2 green chilies
- 1 tsp shrimp paste (optional)
- ¼ cup water

Put all the ingredients in a food processor and process to a paste. Add the toasted spices and process until all the ingredients are well mixed. Store in an airtight container in the refrigerator for up to a week.

NOTE Lemon grass and shrimp paste are available in ethnic stores or sometimes in the ethnic aisle of supermarkets. This curry paste also keeps in the freezer for 6 to 8 weeks.

MAKES ½ CUP

It is neither the ghee—Indian butter—nor the hours and hours of cooking that makes Indian food yummy. It is the turka, which is the base of almost every dish we make. Turka is onions, garlic, ginger, and spices cooked together. Use this sauce with vegetables of your choice; just add the veggies to the sauce and cook until they are done the way you like them.

turka

2 Tbsp grapeseed oil
1 onion, finely chopped
1 Tbsp finely chopped ginger
1 Tbsp finely chopped garlic
1 Tbsp Garam Masala (page 12)
1 tsp ground turmeric
1 tsp salt
1 green chili, finely chopped
2 tomatoes, chopped

Place the oil, onion, ginger, and garlic in a non-stick skillet over medium-high heat and cook for 4 minutes. Stir in the garam masala, turmeric, salt, and chili and cook for 2 minutes. Add the tomatoes and cook for 3 to 5 minutes, stirring regularly.

MAKES ENOUGH FOR A DISH THAT SERVES 3–4

Sambar powder is a mix of spices that comes from the southern part of India. In our small village in the northern part of India, we were not exposed to such spices, so I didn't try sambar powder until I came to Canada, 16 years ago. It brings a uniquely southern flavour to the food because of the asafoetida and curry leaves. If you don't want to make your own, sambar powder is available at Indian grocers.

sambar powder

- 2 Tbsp ground coriander
- 2 Tbsp ground cumin
- 1 Tbsp dried curry leaves, crushed
- 1 tsp whole mustard seeds
- 1 tsp red chili powder
- 1 tsp asafoetida powder
- 1 tsp ground dried ginger
- ½ tsp garlic powder
- ½ tsp ground turmeric
- ¼ tsp mint powder
- ¼ tsp ground cardamom
- ¼ tsp salt

Combine all the ingredients in a bowl and mix well. Store in an airtight container in a cool place for up to 3 months.

NOTE Mint powder can be purchased from ethnic markets, or you can crumble dried mint leaves.

MAKES ABOUT ½ CUP

breads, sauces, and chutneys

In the village, young girls were under enormous pressure to make perfect round thin rotis that fluffed up during cooking. When a new bride went to her in-laws' house on the first day of the wedding, she had to go straight into the kitchen and make a roti to serve to her father-in-law—that's how she was judged to be a good housewife or not. We heard stories of how a bride sometimes hid a perfect roti in her scarf and presented that one. Traditionally, a bride was accompanied by an older female from her side of the family, and it was said that sometimes the elder would secretly make the roti for the bride. Now that I have traumatized my readers with my childhood stories, I would like to share how much fun I have in my kitchen when my husband, daughter, and son make their own rotis. Everyone is covered with flour, and it is all over the kitchen floor.

everyday rotis

2 cups whole wheat flour
¾ cup water

Combine the flour and water in a bowl and knead until it forms a smooth round ball similar to pizza dough, about 2 to 3 minutes. Take a piece of dough about the size of a golf ball and form it into a round shape. Dust your working surface with flour so the dough doesn't stick. Using a rolling pin, roll the dough into a thin patty (like a tortilla).

Place a non-stick skillet over medium heat, and gently place the roti in the pan. When you see some small bubbly spots, flip the roti and cook the other side. When there are brown spots on both sides, the roti is ready.

MAKES 6 ROTIS

This is my signature roti. I invented it when I found out my son might have allergies to processed food. I knew the great health benefits of spinach, broccoli, and lentils, and I wanted him to eat these ingredients every day. Since he is a picky eater, I blend all these into my roti dough. He loves my healthy rotis and eats them with Homemade Yogurt (page 26). I taught my husband, Brad, how to make these, and he takes them on his hiking trips.

bal's healthy rotis

- 2 cups whole wheat flour
- 1 tsp Garam Masala (page 12)
- 1 tsp Chana Masala (page 14)
- ½ tsp salt
- ½ tsp pepper
- ¼ cup fresh or frozen chopped spinach
- ¼ cup finely grated or finely chopped broccoli
- ¼ cup cooked mixed lentils
- ½ Tbsp grated ginger
- ½ cup water (add more if needed)

Combine all the ingredients in a bowl and knead until it has a soft smooth consistency like pizza dough. Take a piece of dough about the size of a golf ball and form it into a round shape. Dust your working surface with flour so the dough doesn't stick. Using a rolling pin, roll the ball into a thin patty (like a tortilla).

Place a non-stick pan over medium heat, and gently place the roti in the pan. When you see some small bubbly spots, flip the roti and cook the other side. When there are brown spots on both sides, the roti is ready.

NOTE Instead of cooking lentils from scratch, use canned lentils and freeze what you don't use for next time.

MAKES 8 ROTIS

Growing up in the village, we cooked our food on a small clay barbecue pit rather than in the traditional tandoor clay oven. Barbecue pits were much safer than tandoors, as it was necessary to put one's hands inside the hot oven to ensure the naan stuck to the oven wall. I was inspired to create this recipe because my daughter, Anoop, loves naan. When her friends come over to visit, they always ask for my healthy naan, too.

whole wheat naan

- 1 cup whole wheat all-purpose flour
- 1 cup whole wheat bread flour
- 1 Tbsp baking powder
- 1 tsp cumin seeds
- 1 tsp salt
- ⅔ cup warm water
- ⅓ cup low-fat plain yogurt at room temperature
- 2 Tbsp flaxseed oil

Place all the ingredients in a bowl and knead until it has a soft smooth consistency like pizza dough. Let it sit on the counter for half an hour and cover it with a plastic wrap. Dust your working surface with flour so the dough doesn't stick. Take a piece of dough about the size of a tennis ball and use a rolling pin to flatten it into an oval shape about 7 to 9 inches long and 4 to 5 inches wide; it should be approximately ¼ inch thick.

Heat the barbecue to medium. Place the naan on the barbecue and cook, turning occasionally, until there are brown spots on each side. Rub a drop of flaxseed oil into the naan to keep it moist. Enjoy!

NOTE You can use 2 cups of whole wheat all-purpose flour if you do not have whole wheat bread flour. If you don't have access to a barbecue, you can use a pizza stone: preheat the stone in the oven at 425°F before cooking the naan. A greased cookie sheet can be used if you do not have a pizza stone.

MAKES 4

Cauliflower parathas are similar to roti, except they are filled with grated cauliflower mixed with various spices. This is my daughter's absolute favourite, and she likes it with Homemade Yogurt (page 26). If it were up to her, she would eat parathas every day. It's hard for her to believe that the only time we had the privilege of eating parathas was when we had guests, and that didn't happen very often because transportation to and from the village was limited. As much as I loved growing up in my village, I tell everyone that I have done my share of living that life. Now I sit on the patio and enjoy the beautiful view of the mountains while I eat my fresh homemade parathas and sip a glass of white wine.

cauliflower-masala parathas

Step 1

1 medium-sized head cauliflower, finely grated
½ cup chopped fresh cilantro
1 green chili, finely chopped
2 Tbsp grated ginger
1 Tbsp Garam Masala (page 12)
1 tsp pomegranate powder
1 tsp salt

Mix all the ingredients until the garam masala is evenly distributed.

Step 2 1 recipe Everyday Rotis dough (page 20)

Take a piece of dough about the size of a golf ball. Dust your working surface with flour so the dough doesn't stick. Using a rolling pin, roll the ball into a thin patty (like a tortilla). Place ¼ cup of the cauliflower mixture in the middle of the patty, fold it over the mixture and form into a small ball.

Dust your working surface with flour again and use a rolling pin to roll the filled ball into a thin patty, incorporating the filling into the dough.

Place a non-stick skillet over medium heat, and gently place the rolled paratha in the pan. When you see some small bubbly spots, flip the paratha and cook the other side. When there are brown spots on both sides, the paratha is ready.

NOTE When you remove the paratha from the pan, place 1 tsp flaxseed oil in the middle and rub it over the surface. The flaxseed oil not only keeps the paratha from drying out, but also adds nutrients. Serve with Sweet Potato Raita (page 27) and Lentil and Split Pea Soup (page 81).

MAKES 6–8 PARATHAS

Homemade yogurt is very flavourful and has no preservatives. My four-year-old son knows when he is eating store-bought yogurt and prefers homemade, maybe because it is filled with mommy love. My daughter often tells me there is no way she is ever leaving home—the food is too good! I think I will be re-evaluating the mommy love when the kids are a bit older.

homemade yogurt

2 cups 2% milk, warmed

2 Tbsp yogurt at room temperature

Preheat the oven to 350°F, and then turn the oven off.

Put the milk in a glass baking dish. Add the yogurt and mix until well combined. Cover with a lid, wrap the dish with a towel, and place in the oven. Let it sit for 6 hours. Remove the towel and refrigerate the yogurt. It will stay fresh for 1 week in the refrigerator.

MAKES 2 CUPS

Raita cools the heat of spicy curry dishes. Traditionally it has deep-fried chickpea flour batter droplets, which I replace with baked sweet potato chunks. Usually, raita is served as a small side dish with the main course.

sweet potato raita

1 cup low-fat sour cream
½ cup skim milk
¼ cup bite-sized pieces cooked sweet potatoes
¼ cup finely chopped red onion
1 Tbsp finely chopped chives
1 tsp Garam Masala (page 12)
½ tsp salt

Place the sour cream and milk in a bowl and whisk until smooth. Add the remaining ingredients and stir well. Leftovers will keep in the refrigerator for 4 or 5 days.

NOTE Cucumber cut into small pieces can replace the sweet potatoes.

SERVES 4

I met Rob Bonas through one of my cooking classes. He is a firefighter in my local community and loves cooking Indian food. His family became testers for my new recipes; his sons Andrew and Trevor inspired me to create more vegetarian dishes. At a private cooking class he asked me to give in his home, we made paneer pakoras, and everyone wanted to learn how to make chutney. It wasn't on the menu, however, and I didn't have any ingredients to make it. When everyone looked a bit disappointed, I asked Rob to get me any kind of canned fruit from his pantry and his lovely wife, Jennifer, to get me some fresh herbs from her organic garden. This recipe is the result.

peach chutney

- one 14 oz can peaches
- 2 Tbsp reserved peach syrup
- ¼ cup chopped red onion
- 1 Tbsp chopped chives or green onions
- 1 green chili, finely chopped
- 1 tsp Chat Masala (page 13)
- ½ tsp salt

Put everything in a blender and mix until the peaches are finely chopped. The chutney will keep in a glass jar in the refrigerator for up to a week. This is delicious with Salmon Paneer Cakes (page 42).

NOTE For additional flavour, add 1 tsp Garam Masala (page 12) and 1 Tbsp chopped cilantro.

MAKES ABOUT 1 CUP

In Punjabi tamarind is called **imli**. *We never ate tamarind chutney by itself. Usually it was used to make mint chutneys or added to dishes such as chickpeas. Now I use it on a regular basis. I like it as a sauce with finger foods, and add it to several dishes for flavour.*

tamarind chutney

2 Tbsp tamarind
½ cup warm water
1 tsp brown sugar
½ tsp red chili powder
½ tsp salt

Combine the tamarind and warm water in a bowl and let it soak for 10 minutes. Use a fork to separate the seeds and the pulp. Strain the water into a bowl. Discard the pulp and seeds.

Mix the sugar, chili powder, and salt into the tamarind water, stirring well. Serve with Baked Samosas (page 38), Paneer Pakoras (page 44), or Turnip Lettuce Wraps (page 48).

MAKES ½ CUP

In our small village, we had no access to fancy fruit such as figs. When I tried them for the first time in Canada, hundreds of recipe ideas came to mind. I could have written an entire cookbook about them! When I discovered that dried figs contain a large amount of calcium and iron, I started using them in my kitchen on a regular basis.

fig chutney

- 1 cup dried figs
- 1 medium red onion
- 1 green chili, finely chopped
- 1 tsp pomegranate powder
- 1 tsp Chat Masala (page 13)
- 1 tsp brown sugar (or raw sugar)
- ½ tsp salt
- ½ cup water

Place all the ingredients in a food processor and process until the figs and onions are coarsely chopped. Use as a dipping sauce for pakoras or wraps.

NOTE Make a date chutney by replacing the figs with dates.

MAKES 1 CUP

My mother made a very special apple chutney for my father, a chutney that only the men in the house were allowed to eat. I sneaked a spoonful occasionally, and one time I was caught. I will not go into details of the consequence, but rest assured I never touched the jar again. I told myself then that when I had my own kitchen I would make this. Let me tell you, this recipe is ten times better than what the men in my household ate!

apple and fig chutney

1 cup chopped apples
1 cup dried figs
¼ cup slivered almonds
¼ cup raisins
1 tsp Chat Masala (page 13)
1 tsp grated ginger
1 cup water

Mix everything in a pot and simmer on low heat for 15 minutes. Let the mixture cool, then place in a food processor and process to a paste. Store in an airtight glass container in the refrigerator for up to a week. Enjoy!

MAKES 1 CUP

Every time I smell ripe mangoes it takes me back to the hot summer days of my childhood. Chocolate wasn't readily available in my village, and mangoes satisfied my sweet tooth. They are still one of my favourite fruits. This chutney is delicious with pakoras, wraps, or tortilla chips. Make sure to serve it chilled.

mango chutney

¼ cup pineapple juice
¼ cup chopped red onion
1 Tbsp chopped fresh cilantro
1 tsp Chat Masala (page 13)
¼ tsp salt
1 cup mango chunks (approx)

Place the juice, onion, cilantro, chat masala, and salt in a food processor and process to a paste. Add the mango and process until the chunks are coarsely chopped. Chill until ready to serve.

NOTE You can vary this by replacing the mangoes with other fresh or canned fruits, such as pineapple or peaches.

MAKES 1 CUP

Mint grew in our garden like a bad weed. We ate mint chutney only during summer. My mom would put all the ingredients in a big round stone bowl and grind them with a thick wooden stick.

mint chutney

- 2 cups washed mint leaves
- 1 medium chili pepper
- ½ cup chopped red onion
- ½ cup chopped fresh cilantro
- 2 Tbsp tamarind water (see page 6)
- 1 Tbsp Garam Masala (page 12)
- 1 tsp salt
- ½ cup water

Place all the ingredients in a food processor and process to a paste. It will keep in an airtight glass container in the refrigerator for up to one week. Use as a dipping sauce for Spinach Pakoras (page 45).

MAKES 1 CUP

finger food and snacks

Since I'm committed to creating a cookbook of healthy recipes, I have to give away my secret recipe for baked samosas—my daughter's favourite lunch. She is in grade ten, and her social life is so important to her that she doesn't want to take any time to sit and eat her lunch. She calls these samosas "lunch to go." With my busy schedule, they are often my ready-to-go lunch as well. They are filled with healthy ingredients, and another plus is that they freeze well—not that there are ever many left to be frozen!

baked samosas

Shell

1 cup whole wheat flour
½ tsp salt
2 Tbsp grapeseed oil
3 Tbsp + 1 tsp water at room temperature

Combine the flour, salt, and oil in a bowl. Mix until the oil is evenly distributed. Mix in the water and knead for 2 to 3 minutes, until it has a smooth consistency like pizza dough. Set aside while you prepare the filling.

Filling

one 14 oz can chickpeas, drained
1 cup cooked brown rice
¼ cup dried cranberries
1 Tbsp Garam Masala (page 12)
2 tsp cumin seeds
1 tsp red chili flakes
1 tsp ground dried ginger
1 tsp salt

Mix all the ingredients gently in a large bowl until the garam masala is evenly distributed.

To make the samosas

- ¼ cup water in a small bowl
- 2 Tbsp grapeseed oil

Preheat the oven to 425°F.

Divide the dough into 4 pieces and form each into a ball. Take 1 piece of dough and form it into a round flat shape. Dust your working surface with flour so the dough doesn't stick. Using a rolling pin, roll the dough into a thin patty (like a tortilla). Cut the circle in half.

Take 1 half-circle and make a cone shape. Wet the edges with a little water to glue the overlapping edges together. Put ¼ cup of filling in the cone. Moisten the top of the inside edges and close the cone, pressing the edges to seal it. Brush the grapeseed oil on each side of the samosa and place on a baking sheet. Repeat with the remaining ingredients.

Place in the preheated oven and bake for 10 to 12 minutes, then flip the samosas and bake for another 5 minutes, or until the samosas are nicely browned. Serve with chutney (see pages 28 to 35).

NOTE I tried cooking samosas on the barbecue on medium heat, and it worked very well.

MAKES 8 SAMOSAS

This simple recipe was one of the favourites when I had a small catering business specializing in finger food. You will need six metal skewers to make the kabobs.

indian-thai lamb kabobs

2 lb lamb shoulder
1 cup low-fat plain yogurt
½ cup Fusion Curry Paste (page 15)

Cut the lamb into 1-inch cubes. Place the yogurt and curry paste in a large bowl and mix until the ingredients are well combined. Add the lamb and stir until the lamb is well coated with the mixture. Cover and refrigerate for 45 minutes or up to 5 hours.

Heat a barbecue to medium. Slide the meat on metal skewers. Gently place the skewers on the heat and cook until the meat is pale pink inside and brown outside, about 4 to 6 minutes, turning frequently. Use one of my chutneys for a dipping sauce (see pages 28 to 35); the Paneer Dressing (page 72) is nice too.

NOTE You can also use bamboo skewers for the kabobs, but make sure to soak them in warm water for at least 5 minutes before cooking so they won't burn. If you don't like or have access to lamb, pork tenderloin is a good substitute.

MAKES 6 SKEWERS

Paneer is Punjabi homemade cheese. Even though we had bison and cows in our backyard, my mother never made paneer. The only time we had it was at big social functions such as weddings. At a cooking class I gave, a couple from Mexico told me they had an item similar to paneer—queso blanco—that was used as dessert. They would cut the cheese into smaller chunks, soak them with brown sugar and whipping cream, and bake them for 15 minutes. Here is the recipe for paneer; please feel free to experiment with it. Homemade paneer is always better, but you can also purchase it from an ethnic market. You can serve this as an appetizer with a chutney of your choice (see pages 28 to 35).

homemade paneer

1 gallon (4 litres) 2% milk
½ cup plain white vinegar
one 20-inch-square piece of cheesecloth

Bring the milk to a boil in a large pot. Add the vinegar and stir until the mixture separates into solids and liquid. Drain the mixture through cheesecloth. Wrap the curd with the cheesecloth, place in a sieve, and put a heavy weight on it, such as a cookie jar or rice container. Let the water drain completely for 20 minutes.

Remove the cheesecloth and cut the paneer into small cubes. Use immediately or refrigerate in a covered container for up to 5 days.

NOTE Pan-frying helps to keep the paneer cubes from falling apart. Place 2 Tbsp grapeseed oil in a non-stick pan over medium heat. When the oil is hot, gently place the paneer in the pan and cook until golden brown. Gently flip the pieces and brown the other side. Pan-fried paneer freezes and thaws very well without crumbling.

MAKES ABOUT 1 LB

Since I grew up as a vegetarian far from the coast, I never had an opportunity to try any seafood. I tasted salmon for the first time in one of the fanciest restaurants in Vancouver and could not believe how it just melted in my mouth. Since salmon also has great nutritional value, I created a few recipes for this book. Keep canned salmon in the pantry so you can make this when guests arrive unexpectedly and you don't have time to run to the store. Serve these with Mint Chutney (page 35), Peach Chutney (page 28), or Yam and Red Onion Chutney (page 32).

salmon paneer cakes

- one 6 oz can salmon, drained and liquid squeezed out
- ¾ cup Homemade Paneer (page 41), grated
- ¼ cup low-fat plain yogurt
- ¼ cup finely chopped red onion
- ¼ cup chickpea flour
- 1 tsp Garam Masala (page 12)
- ½ tsp salt
- 2 Tbsp grapeseed oil

Combine all the ingredients except the oil in a bowl and mix until the flour is evenly distributed. Make small cakes (1-inch patties). Heat the oil in a non-stick skillet over medium heat and pan-fry the patties on both sides until golden brown.

NOTE Adding 1 tsp of dried fenugreek leaves, 1 tsp of Chana Masala (page 14), and 1 Tbsp of finely chopped ginger gives an enticing aroma to the cakes. You can also sprinkle fresh lemon juice over the cakes just before serving to brighten all of the flavours.

MAKES 6–8 CAKES

This is another quick and easy finger food. Paneer can be bought from any Indian grocer in one-pound bricks, although homemade paneer is always better (see page 41; double the recipe to make these pakoras). I also serve these pakoras on top of a green salad for a delicious first course.

paneer pakoras

- 1 cup chickpea flour
- 1 tsp fenugreek leaves
- 1 tsp Chana Masala (page 14)
- ½ tsp Spanish paprika
- ½ tsp salt
- ¼ cup water (approx)
- 1 lb solid paneer
- 2 Tbsp grapeseed oil

Mix the chickpea flour, fenugreek, chana masala, paprika, and salt together in a bowl. Add enough water to give the mixture the consistency of pancake batter.

Cut the paneer into thin slices and dip each slice in the mixture. Heat the oil in a non-stick pan over medium-high heat. Pan-fry the paneer on both sides until golden brown. Serve with chutney (see pages 28 to 35).

NOTE These pakoras are great for stuffing wraps. Place 5 pakoras in the middle of a whole wheat tortilla, and add ½ cup chopped lettuce and 1 Tbsp chutney. Wrap it gently and you have a perfect take-out lunch. The wraps freeze well, too!

MAKES 12–16 PAKORAS

When I was growing up, the arrival of guests was exciting, because that was when my mother made fancy dishes. Now I understand why she cooked this only on special occasions: she deep-fried the pakoras in oil, an item that was scarce, and we could not afford to cook like that on a daily basis. These pakoras freeze very well.

spinach pakoras

- 2 cups frozen spinach, thawed and the water squeezed out
- ½ cup plain yogurt
- ½ cup finely chopped red onion
- ½ cup chickpea flour
- 1 tsp fenugreek leaves
- 1 tsp Garam Masala (page 12)
- 1 tsp salt
- 2 Tbsp grapeseed oil

Mix all the ingredients except the oil together until well combined. Form into small balls that are about half the size of a golf ball.

Place the oil in a non-stick skillet over medium-high heat. Put as many pakoras as you can in the pan; they can be touching each other, but shouldn't be overcrowded. Cook them on all sides until golden brown. Serve with Mango Chutney (page 34) or Mint Chutney (page 35).

NOTE Add 1 Tbsp grated ginger to give a little bit of heat and a distinctive flavour that complements the other spices. If you don't have fresh ginger, use 1 tsp ground ginger.

MAKES 10–14 PAKORAS

***Gobi** means "cauliflower" in Punjabi. **Koftas** are round balls filled with various ingredients, and the end product looks like meatballs. This dish was invented from ingredients left over from making homemade pizza. (Now, you might wonder why anyone would put cauliflower on pizza. My crazy inspirations come from a pizza place at the student union building at the University of British Columbia—the stuff they put on the pizzas was unbelievable!) Getting back to the recipe, after I finished making my cauliflower pizza, I didn't want to put the rest of the ingredients back in the refrigerator and decided to make these cauliflower balls. My daughter and her teenaged friends liked them very much. I knew I had a winner.*

mozzarella gobi koftas

1 cup finely grated cauliflower
¼ cup grated mozzarella cheese
2 Tbsp chickpea flour
2 Tbsp low-fat plain yogurt
1 tsp Garam Masala (page 12)
½ tsp salt
2 Tbsp grapeseed oil

In a bowl, combine all the ingredients except the oil and mix well. Form into small balls. Place the oil in a non-stick skillet over medium-high heat, add the balls and cook them on all sides until golden brown. Serve with Sweet Potato Raita (page 27).

MAKES 6–8 KOFKAS

Occasionally I make these flavourful yam cakes instead of potato patties. They're fine gourmet treats to serve guests. Use them to top a green salad, or serve the cakes with an assortment of chutneys (see pages 28 to 35).

yam cakes

- 2 cups cooked and mashed yams
- ½ cup chickpea flour
- ¼ cup chopped fresh cilantro
- 2 Tbsp low-fat plain yogurt
- 1 Tbsp Garam Masala (page 12)
- 1 Tbsp grated ginger
- 1 tsp salt
- 2 Tbsp grapeseed oil

Mix the yams, chickpea flour, cilantro, yogurt, garam masala, ginger, and salt in a bowl until well blended. Form into small round patties. Heat the oil in a non-stick pan over medium-high heat. Cook the patties in batches so they have plenty of room and aren't touching in the pan. Cook on each side until golden brown, about 2 minutes per side.

MAKES 14 CAKES

I love Szechuan-style Chinese food, but I cannot cook it at home because my son has severe peanut allergies, and the dishes often contain peanuts. At a Szechuan restaurant, I always order the lettuce wraps, and the usual choices are chicken, beef, or pork. Wondering what vegetarians would eat if they wanted lettuce wraps inspired me to create this version.

turnip lettuce wraps

- 2 Tbsp grapeseed oil
- 1 large onion, chopped
- 1 Tbsp finely chopped ginger
- 1 Tbsp finely chopped garlic
- 1 Tbsp cumin seeds
- 1 tsp mustard seeds
- 2 medium turnips, grated
- ¼ cup thinly sliced chives or green onions
- ¼ tsp salt
- ¼ cup Tamarind Chutney (page 29)
- 1 head butter lettuce

Place the oil in a non-stick skillet over medium heat, add the onion, ginger, and garlic, and cook for 4 minutes. Add the cumin and mustard seeds, and cook for 1 minute. Add the turnips, chives, and salt, reduce the heat to medium-low and cook for 3 to 5 minutes, stirring regularly.

To serve, place ¼ cup of the mixture and 1 Tbsp of chutney in a large lettuce leaf. Wrap the lettuce around the mixture and enjoy!

NOTE You can vary the recipe by adding a few more spices, such as 1 Tbsp fenugreek leaves, 1 tsp Spanish paprika, or a finely chopped green chili.

SERVES 4

At numerous cooking classes over the last eight years, people have come to me at the end of class and requested recipes for healthy vegetarian food. This recipe is a great vegetarian finger food for parties, and my daughter tells me that when I pack these quesadillas in her lunch, her friends always want to trade their food for hers.

vegetarian quesadillas

- 2 Tbsp grapeseed oil
- 1 cup thinly sliced zucchini
- 1 cup thinly sliced portobello mushrooms
- 1 Tbsp grated ginger
- 1 cup cooked lentils, drained
- 2 Tbsp Chana Masala (page 14)
- 6 whole wheat tortillas
- 1 cup grated low-fat mozzarella cheese

Place the oil, zucchini, mushrooms, and ginger in a non-stick skillet and cook on medium heat until the zucchini is tender, about 5 minutes. Add the lentils and chana masala, and cook for 2 more minutes. Turn the heat off.

Preheat the oven to 425°F. Place a tortilla on a baking sheet. Put one-third of the mixture in the middle and spread it evenly to cover the tortilla. Sprinkle ⅓ cup of the cheese evenly over the mixture. Place another tortilla on top and press it gently. Repeat with the remaining ingredients.

Place the baking sheet in the oven and bake until the cheese melts, about 3 to 5 minutes. Cut into 6 wedges with a pizza cutter and serve with chutney (see pages 28 to 35).

NOTE For more protein, you can add grated extra-firm tofu to the mixture with the zucchini and mushrooms. For additional flavour, add a finely chopped red onion, 1 Tbsp Garam Masala (page 12), and 1 tsp Spanish paprika.

MAKES 18 PIECES

Chickpeas are high in calcium, and this dip is a staple in our house. Serve it with raw vegetables or tortilla chips. It's also great for lunch wraps: place a tablespoon of the chickpea dip on a whole wheat tortilla, add a few pieces of deli meat, and top with some grated cucumber and carrot. This is another recipe you can experiment with.

chickpea dip

one 14 oz can chickpeas, drained
1 red onion, coarsely chopped
1 green chili, chopped
1 tsp Chat Masala (page 13)
½ tsp ground coriander
½ tsp ground cumin
1 tsp finely grated garlic
1 tsp salt
¼ cup water

Put everything in a food processor and process to a smooth texture. Leftovers will keep covered in the refrigerator for 5 days.

NOTE Add 1 Tbsp cilantro and ¼ cup toasted cashews for additional flavour.

MAKES 1 CUP

salads and dressings

The first time I ate an organic ripe papaya, I thought I had gone to heaven, and right then I knew I had to create some dishes with it. Papaya is very flavourful and has great health benefits; it contains beta-carotene, calcium, vitamin A and C, flavonoids, and folate, and it has anti-inflammatory properties. If you have leftover rice from the day before, it is perfect for this recipe. This is great for summer meals on the patio.

fresh papaya, green pea, and rice salad

- 2 Tbsp grapeseed oil
- 1 tsp mustard seeds
- 1 tsp cumin seeds
- 1 Tbsp Garam Masala (page 12)
- 1 tsp salt
- 1 cup green peas (frozen)
- 2 cups papaya, peeled and cut into bite-sized pieces
- 1 cup cooked brown basmati rice
- ¼ cup cooked wild rice
- 2 tsp Chat Masala (page 13)
- 1 tsp fresh lime juice

Combine the oil, mustard seeds, and cumin seeds in a non-stick skillet and cook over medium-high heat for 10 seconds. Add the garam masala and salt and cook for 10 seconds. Stir in the green peas and cook until tender, about 3 minutes. Remove from the heat and let the mixture cool.

Add the papaya, brown rice, wild rice, chat masala, and lime juice. Mix everything gently. Enjoy!

NOTE If papaya is unavailable, use any tropical fruit that you love.

SERVES 4

White radish is called **mooli** *in Punjabi. It's white, of course, and is shaped like a carrot. It has a sweet turnip-like flavour. This was the only salad we ate when we were growing up. After eating fresh organic cucumber for 20 years, when I first came to Canada and tried a cucumber, it made me very sad. I was sad not only because the tasteless cucumbers were sold to people, but also because I had to live in Canada for the rest of my life eating these cucumbers. Luckily, many grocery stores have begun embracing organic food.*

simple cucumber and white radish salad

1 medium-sized cucumber
1 medium-sized white radish
1 tsp lime juice
pinch salt
pinch black pepper

Chop the cucumber and radish into 1-inch chunks. Combine all the ingredients in a large bowl and let sit for 5 minutes before serving.

SERVES 4

Rapini is a green leafy vegetable that is rich in calcium and iron. In the village, we grew it during winter, and as I hand-picked each stem, I would nibble on the tender, flavourful raw rapini. My mother would cook the greens on low heat for hours. When I came here, I learned that leafy greens should not be cooked for a long time because it destroys the nutrients, and I use steaming as a cooking technique so we can enjoy the health benefits.

rapini and bocconcini salad

1 lb rapini
2 medium low-fat bocconcini balls
2 Tbsp flaxseed oil
½ tsp finely grated garlic
½ tsp Chat Masala (page 13)
½ tsp salt
1 pkg thin dried rice noodles

Steam the rapini until tender. Cut the bocconcini into cubes. In a bowl whisk the oil, garlic, chat masala, and salt together.

Fill a pot with hot water and soak the noodles for 2 minutes or until they are tender. Strain the noodles and place on a platter. Top with the rapini and bocconcini and sprinkle the dressing on top before serving. Enjoy!

NOTE You can replace the bocconcini with extra-firm organic tofu, which I like to lightly pan-fry. Rapini is sometimes sold as broccoli raab.

SERVES 4

When I create recipes, some are inspired by my childhood experiences, some are inspired by the fruit and vegetable aisle of a grocery store, some are accidental discoveries, and some are just because I like to see different colours on the plate. In this recipe not only do the organic cherry tomatoes taste like candies, but they also have a gorgeous rich colour. This is another very quick recipe, especially since I always use leftover paneer from other dishes to make the salad.

cherry tomato and paneer salad

- 20 cherry tomatoes
- 1 cup bite-sized pieces of Homemade Paneer (see page 41), pan-fried
- ½ cup toasted pecan halves
- 2 Tbsp flaxseed oil
- 1 Tbsp Chat Masala (page 13)
- 1 Tbsp lemon juice
- 1 Tbsp finely chopped mint
- 1 tsp warm honey

Put all the ingredients in a large salad bowl. Mix everything until the chat masala is evenly distributed. Enjoy!

NOTE I substitute various seeds for the nuts because my son is allergic.

SERVES 4

We had one pomegranate tree in our village. When the pomegranates were ready, it was hard to see any leaves because the tree would be covered with red hanging balls, just like a Christmas tree. My mom dried the seeds under the sun and used them for chutneys and other dishes. This is a great patio party salad. If you don't like the crunchiness of the pomegranate seeds, replace them with pitted cherries.

tofu pomegranate salad

- 1 lb extra-firm organic tofu
- 2 Tbsp grapeseed oil
- 1 Tbsp soy sauce
- 1 Tbsp Chana Masala (page 14)
- ¼ cup fresh pomegranate seeds
- 1 Tbsp lemon juice
- 1 Tbsp flaxseed oil

Cut the tofu into thin rectangular pieces. Place the oil and tofu in a non-stick skillet over medium heat and cook until each side of the tofu is golden brown, about 2 minutes. Add the soy sauce and sprinkle the chana masala over the tofu pieces. Cook for 30 seconds, moving or flipping regularly. Set aside to cool.

Combine the pomegranate seeds, lemon juice, and flaxseed oil in a large bowl. Pour over the tofu and toss to combine. Serve with Vegetarian Quesadillas (page 52).

SERVES 4

We have a very small aluminum boat we use for fishing. Since it's small, I try not to take too much with me, but past experience has taught me that once we are on the water it is very hard to convince my husband, Brad, to return ashore unless he has caught a fish. It used to be that Anoop and I would complain, and Brad and Aaron would be in heaven. Now Anoop and I have a perfect plan—we bring along our manicure and pedicure kits, the gossip magazines, and sometimes even our portable DVD player. This way we are still together having "family fun" and are not ready to kill each other. I often make this salad to take with us in a small cooler because it is filling, yummy, and quick to make. Kidney beans take a long time to cook, so I always keep canned kidney beans in my pantry.

kidney beans with goat cheese

- one 14 oz can kidney beans, drained
- one 14 oz can haricot beans, drained
- 1 cup chopped tomatoes
- 1 cup finely chopped red onion
- ½ cup cubed goat cheese
- 2 Tbsp flaxseed oil
- 1 Tbsp lemon juice
- 1 tsp Chat Masala (page 13)
- 1 tsp mango powder
- ½ tsp salt
- ½ tsp pepper

Put everything in a salad bowl and gently mix until the chat masala and mango powder are evenly distributed.

SERVES 4

On hot summer days, I don't usually feel like eating a big meal, and salads are a good choice, especially if they have protein. I try to use seasonal food as much as possible, and summer brings lots of fantastic fruit and vegetables to choose from.

mango chicken salad

- 2 Tbsp grapeseed oil
- 1 Tbsp finely chopped ginger
- 1 Tbsp finely chopped garlic
- 1 Tbsp Garam Masala (page 12)
- 1 lb boneless, skinless chicken breast, cut into bite-sized pieces
- 1 green chili, finely chopped
- 1 tsp salt
- 1 cup bite-sized mango chunks
- 1 head butter lettuce, washed and chopped

Place the oil, ginger, garlic, and garam masala in a non-stick skillet and cook over medium-high heat for 2 minutes. Add the chicken, green chili, and salt, and cook on medium heat, stirring regularly, until the chicken is cooked through, about 9 to 12 minutes. Remove from the heat, transfer the chicken to a bowl, and cool in the refrigerator.

Combine the chicken and mango chunks. Serve over a bed of lettuce.

NOTE To vary the flavours, add ½ cup chopped cilantro and ½ cup toasted cashews.

SERVES 4

Back when I was working on my Master of Education degree, my friend Louise came by one time to go over some of our assigned readings. I didn't have anything planned for our lunch, so I gathered a few things from my pantry and the fridge and created this dish. She asked for the recipe, and my response was, "What recipe?" She looked at me and said, "You would be an absolute crazy woman if you didn't write this recipe down." I told her that if I started writing down every single recipe I created, I'd have ten books written by now. She didn't care that I was joking around and made sure that not only did I write it down, but also included it in my first cookbook.

mustard thai chicken salad

2 Tbsp grapeseed oil
1 Tbsp grated garlic
1 Tbsp mustard seeds
1 lb boneless, skinless chicken breast, cut into small bite-sized pieces
¼ cup low-fat coconut milk
¼ cup Thai sweet and sour sauce
1 lb mixed salad greens

Place the oil and garlic in a non-stick skillet over medium-high heat and cook for 20 seconds. Add the mustard seeds and cook for 20 seconds, stirring. Add the chicken and cook over medium heat until it's almost cooked through, about 8 minutes. Add the coconut milk and Thai sauce, and cook over medium-low heat until the chicken is fully cooked, about 2 minutes.

Arrange the greens on 4 plates and mound the chicken on top of the greens.

NOTE You could turn this into a meal by serving the chicken over rice or cooked Thai noodles with a green salad on the side.

SERVES 4

When Anoop was 13 years old, she went through a prawn phase. She often requested prawns for dinner, and I told her that she should start experimenting with some of my spices and create her own prawn dishes. Much to my surprise, she went through my spice cabinet and pulled out the ingredients below. The only things I added to her list were the garlic and flaxseed oil. She wrote down the recipe as I cooked so she could make it herself later on and impress her friends. At the end of the meal, Anoop suggested that since she participated in creating this recipe, I should name it "Anoop's Prawn Salad." I told her I didn't have a problem with it as long as her room was spotless; otherwise I would not consider her request. As you can see, the name is not changed . . . love thy teenagers!

limed prawns

- 2 Tbsp grapeseed oil
- 1 Tbsp grated garlic
- 1 tsp fenugreek leaves
- 1 tsp Spanish paprika
- 1 tsp Garam Masala (page 12)
- 1 tsp Chana Masala (page 14)
- 20 prawns, peeled
- 1 Tbsp lime juice
- 1 head lettuce, washed and chopped
- 2 Tbsp flaxseed oil

Place the oil and garlic in a non-stick skillet and cook over medium-high heat for 20 seconds. Add the fenugreek leaves, paprika, garam masala, and chana masala, and cook for 1 minute, stirring regularly. Mix in the prawns and cook over medium-low heat for 3 to 5 minutes. Stir in the lime juice and cook for 30 seconds.

Arrange the chopped lettuce on 4 plates and place the prawns on top. Sprinkle with flaxseed oil before serving.

NOTE For a vegetarian dish, replace the prawns with a 14 oz can of chickpeas and a can of water chestnuts.

SERVES 4

My first tuna experience was with sushi, and I absolutely loved it. In this dish you can still taste the tuna, along with the great flavours of cumin and coriander.

tuna with greens

- ¼ tsp ground cumin
- ¼ tsp ground coriander
- ¼ tsp Spanish paprika
- pinch salt
- ½ lb fresh tuna fillet, 1½ inches thick
- 1 tsp grapeseed oil
- 1 lb mixed salad greens
- Basic Lemon Dressing (page 73)
- ¼ cup pomegranate seeds (optional)

Combine the cumin, coriander, paprika, and salt in a bowl. Place the tuna in the bowl and coat it with the spices.

Heat the oil in a non-stick skillet over medium to high heat. Gently place the tuna in the pan, and sear it on each spiced side for about 20 seconds.

Remove from the heat. Slice the tuna thinly with a sharp knife. Distribute the greens among four plates, arrange the tuna slices on top, and drizzle with the dressing. Top with pomegranate seeds.

SERVES 4

I have never been crazy about store-bought dressings, maybe because I'm not used to them. A fresh salad dressing takes less than two minutes to make, it's delicious, and it has no preservatives. I have used this dressing in several of my cooking classes, and it always gets rave reviews.

mango dressing

- ¼ cup mango juice
- 3 Tbsp flaxseed oil or extra virgin olive oil
- 2 Tbsp finely chopped mango
- 1 Tbsp lemon juice
- 1 Tbsp finely chopped fresh cilantro (optional)
- ¼ tsp Garam Masala (page 12)
- pinch salt and pepper

Combine all of the ingredients, and the dressing is ready. Serve it over greens. Refrigerate leftovers in a glass jar for up to 5 days.

NOTE I like to use this dressing over organic spinach topped with thinly sliced mangoes.

MAKES ABOUT ½ CUP

LEFT TO RIGHT Basic Lemon Dressing (page 73), Raspberry and Red Wine Vinaigrette (page 76), and Mango Dressing (facing page)

Every Saturday during summer there is a farmers' market in Vancouver where all sorts of organic berries are sold. Last summer, I went a little too crazy with my berry shopping. At the end of the spree, my truck was full of strawberries, raspberries, and blueberries. My husband, daughter, and son all pitched in to help wash the berries and individually freeze them. We sat on our patio and ran the garden hose and had a great family time. Everyone was eating the strawberries and blueberries, but no one was touching the raspberries, so I knew I had to do something with them or they would be in the freezer for a long time. This is one of the recipes I came up with.

raspberry and red wine vinaigrette

- 1 cup frozen raspberries, thawed
- 2 Tbsp red wine vinegar
- 1 tsp grated garlic
- 1 tsp Chat Masala (page 13)
- ½ tsp salt
- ½ tsp pepper
- ¼ cup flaxseed oil

Put the ingredients in a deep bowl and whisk until the dressing is well combined. This will keep in a glass jar in the refrigerator for up to 5 days.

NOTE Although it sounds like an unusual combination, everyone likes this dressing drizzled over a fresh tomato and basil salad.

MAKES 1¼ CUPS

soups

This creamy soup is made with gently blanched cauliflower and infused with traditional Punjabi spices. The milk softens the spices, creating a full yet subtle flavour. My son, who normally is not too crazy about cauliflower, has no complaints whenever I make this.

no-cream cauliflower soup

- 1 head medium cauliflower, chopped
- 2½ cups water
- 2 Tbsp grapeseed oil
- 1 Tbsp grated ginger
- 1 tsp cumin seeds
- 1 tsp Chana Masala (page 14)
- 1½ tsp salt
- ¼ cup 2% milk

Bring the cauliflower and water to a boil, then simmer on low heat until tender, about 4 minutes. Take off the heat and let cool a bit. Using a blender, process until creamy. Put the soup back into the pot and return to a boil. Combine the oil, ginger, cumin seeds, chana masala, and salt in a non-stick skillet over medium heat and cook for 2 minutes. Stir in the cauliflower mixture and cook for 30 seconds. Turn the heat off and stir in the milk. Enjoy!

NOTE You can replace the milk with soy or rice milk. When using organic cauliflower, wash it thoroughly before steaming to get rid of any insects—otherwise it would not be a vegetarian dish!

SERVES 4

When my mother cooked lentils, she would first put them on a large tray and go through them one at a time to pick out the rocks. Then she would wash the lentils until the water ran clear to get rid of the dirt. I still go through lentils almost one at a time before rinsing them. When Brad saw me doing that, I'm sure he thought I had lost it, and, trust me, it was not the first time he had wondered about my unusual kitchen behaviours. One day he said to me, "Honey, no offence . . . but what are you looking for in the lentils?" I looked at him with amazement and said, "Rocks." He said packaged lentils are always clean. I told him I was very sure that when farmers picked them it was not a priority that the lentils be dirt free. He still thinks I have unusual practices when it comes to food and cooking, but after ten years we are still together, so I guess it can't be that bad.

lentil and split pea soup

- 1 cup brown lentils
- ¼ cup split peas
- 5 cups water
- 2 Tbsp grapeseed oil
- 2 Tbsp grated garlic
- 1 Tbsp grated ginger
- 1 Tbsp cumin seeds
- 1 Tbsp Garam Masala (page 12)
- 1 tsp salt

Go through the lentils and split peas to ensure there are no rocks. Wash them until the water runs clear. Bring the lentils, split peas, and water to a boil in a large pot. Reduce the heat to low and let the lentils simmer until cooked, about 30 minutes. When they are cooked, you should be able to mash the lentils and the split peas with a fork.

In a separate pan, cook the oil, garlic, and ginger over medium-high heat for 2 minutes. Stir in the cumin seeds, garam masala, and salt, and cook for 2 minutes on medium heat. Add the mixture to the lentils and simmer for 2 minutes. Turn the heat off and cover with a lid. Let sit for 10 minutes before serving.

NOTE There are many kinds of lentils and some cook faster than others. To learn more about lentils and their cooking time, check my website: www.balshealthykitchen.com.

SERVES 4

I was introduced to various new vegetables, including beets, when I first came to Canada. I quickly determined never to wear a white shirt when cooking beets because the gorgeous red hue can stain anything. On a visit to my mother-in-law, Donna, I noticed she was using beet water to dye her handspun wool. Boiling beets with the skins on helps retain the rich colour. This soup makes a great gourmet start to a fancy meal.

beet soup

- 2 large beets, peeled and chopped
- 2 cups water (or enough to cover the beets)
- 2 Tbsp grapeseed oil
- 1 large onion, chopped
- 1 Tbsp grated ginger
- 1 Tbsp Garam Masala (page 12)
- ¼ tsp salt
- ¼ cup low-fat sour cream (optional)

Put the beets in a saucepan and add the water. Cook the beets over medium heat for 10 to 12 minutes. Remove from the heat and cool slightly (do not drain). Put the beets and the water in a food processor and process until smooth.

While the beets are cooking, heat the oil in a non-stick skillet over medium heat. Add the onion and ginger and cook for 4 minutes. Add the garam masala and salt and cook for 2 minutes. Stir in the pureéd beet mixture and remove from the heat.

Ladle the soup into 4 bowls and place 1 Tbsp of sour cream in the middle of each serving, if desired.

SERVES 4

My mother would throw yams in the barbecue pit after cooking a meal, and the yams would slowly roast on the coals. Then she would put some butter and sugar on them and we would have them for dessert. This flavourful yam soup has a soothing creamy texture and is enhanced with a touch of South Indian spices.

soothing yam soup

- 1 lb yams, peeled and cubed
- 3½ cups water
- 2 Tbsp grapeseed oil
- 1 Tbsp Sambar Powder (page 17)
- 1 tsp cumin seeds
- ½ tsp salt
- ½ tsp pepper

Cook the yams in water over medium heat until tender, 7 to 9 minutes. Transfer to a blender and process until creamy.

Place oil, sambar powder, cumin seeds, and salt in a non-stick skillet over medium-low heat and cook for 20 seconds. Add the spice mixture to the yams and mix until the spices are evenly distributed.

NOTE I intended this soup to have the consistency of clam chowder. If it's too thick, add a little more water while you're blending the yams.

SERVES 4

Growing up I used to call split peas "half chickpeas," but the actual Punjabi name was **dalvain cholai,** *which I could never remember. When I was nine I found out that if you pronounced chickpeas as a singular word, it meant the male reproductive organ in Punjabi. I would purposely pronounce it that way, pretending I didn't know what it meant, just to see my aunt giggle. My great-great-grand-aunt always giggled and shushed me immediately even though there was no one else around. She made the best split peas, and I always licked my bowl at the end. She would then remind me that it was only acceptable for men to do such a thing—I was constantly reminded that men were considered superior and allowed to get away with all kinds of things! Getting back to the soup . . . I always receive great feedback after people (men and women) try out this recipe.*

split pea and tofu soup

2 Tbsp grapeseed oil
2 Tbsp grated ginger
2 Tbsp grated garlic
1 Tbsp Garam Masala (page 12)
1 tsp ground turmeric
1 tsp salt
1 cup dried split peas
one 14 oz can crushed tomatoes
6 cups water
1 lb extra-firm organic tofu, cubed
2 Tbsp grapeseed oil

Place the oil, ginger, and garlic in a non-stick skillet over medium-high heat and cook for 2 minutes. Add the garam masala, ground turmeric, and salt, and cook for 3 minutes, stirring regularly. Add the split peas, tomatoes, and water and bring to a boil. Reduce the heat to low and simmer until the split peas are cooked, about 30 to 40 minutes.

While the split peas are cooking, cook the tofu in oil in a non-stick pan over medium heat until all sides are golden brown, about 3 minutes. When the split peas are done, add the tofu chunks to the soup. Let the soup sit for 10 minutes before serving.

NOTE Pan-fried paneer can be used if organic tofu is not available. For Homemade Paneer see page 41.

SERVES 4

vegetable dishes

Rajmanh *is the name for red kidney beans. Usually my mother cooked them on cold winter days; the coals of the barbecue pit would heat the room up while it kept a big pot of beans slowly cooking. In my kitchen, I sometimes use canned kidney beans for this recipe, but on many occasions, I have cooked a big pot of raw beans by covering them with boiling water, soaking them overnight, and simmering them the next day. If you use canned beans, drain them well before adding them to the dish.*

kidney bean masala

- 2 Tbsp grapeseed oil
- 1 tsp asafoetida
- 1 large onion, finely chopped
- 2 Tbsp chopped garlic
- 2 Tbsp grated ginger
- 1 Tbsp tomato paste
- 1 Tbsp curry leaves
- 1 Tbsp cumin seeds
- 1 Tbsp Garam Masala (page 12)
- 1 tsp ground turmeric
- 1 tsp Spanish paprika
- 1 tsp salt
- 1 cup crushed tomatoes
- 1 cup water
- one 14 oz can kidney beans, drained

Place the oil and asafoetida in a non-stick skillet over medium-high heat and cook for 5 seconds. Add the onion, garlic, and ginger and cook for 4 minutes. Add the tomato paste, curry leaves, cumin, garam masala, turmeric, paprika, and salt and cook for 2 minutes.

Stir in the crushed tomatoes and water, bring the sauce to a boil, lower the heat to a simmer, and cook for 10 minutes. Add the kidney beans and cook for 2 minutes. Serve with rice or plain rotis (see page 20).

SERVES 4

Fresh vegetables are always best, of course, but I learned that frozen veggies have the same nutritional value. The benefit of frozen spinach is that it's pre-washed and tightly packed together. Having it on hand in the freezer is also a bonus. This dish is made on a regular basis in my kitchen because spinach is a great source of calcium and iron.

spinach and green peas

- 2 Tbsp grapeseed oil
- 2 Tbsp grated ginger
- 2 Tbsp grated garlic
- 1 green chili, chopped
- 1 tsp Garam Masala (page 12)
- 1 tsp salt
- 1 tomato, chopped
- 1 cup frozen peas
- 1 lb frozen spinach, thawed

Combine the oil, ginger, and garlic in a non-stick skillet over medium-high heat and cook for 2 minutes. Stir in the green chili, garam masala, and salt, and cook for 1 minute. Add the tomato and cook for 2 minutes. Stir in the peas and spinach, reduce the heat to medium-low, and cook until the peas are tender, about 3 minutes. Serve with rice or plain rotis (see page 20).

SERVES 4

Traditionally this dish is called **saag**, *and it is cooked for a long time. We only ate it in winter and we had it with corn flour rotis and white radish salad. I add broccoli to the dish and steam the greens so I can retain the nutrients.*

steamed rapini and broccoli with paneer

- 2 cups chopped broccoli
- 2 cups chopped rapini
- 1 package frozen spinach, thawed
- 1 green chili, chopped
- ¾ cup water
- 2 Tbsp grapeseed oil
- 1 onion, chopped
- 1 Tbsp finely chopped garlic
- 1 Tbsp finely chopped ginger
- 1 Tbsp Garam Masala (page 12)
- 1 tsp salt
- 1 cup cubed Homemade Paneer (page 41), pan-fried

Steam the broccoli and rapini until tender. Place them in a food processor with the thawed spinach, green chili, and water and process to a paste.

Combine the oil, onion, garlic, and ginger in a non-stick skillet over medium-high heat and cook for 4 minutes. Add the garam masala and salt and cook for 1 minute. Stir in the paneer and the rapini purée and simmer for 2 minutes on low heat. Serve with rice or plain rotis (see page 20).

NOTE Rapini is sometimes sold as broccoli raab.

SERVES 4

When I found out that a lovely woman named Irine, who was 74 years old, could not get into my cooking classes because they were always full, I decided to give a private cooking class to a few wonderful ladies at Irine's home. Irine travels all over the world and loves eating all kinds of food. I made this dish not knowing that she couldn't stand chickpeas and asked her to taste it for me. Brave Irine got up and tried a spoonful, and the first thing that came out of her mouth was, "I don't like chickpeas, but I can eat this entire pot." I'm now her adopted granddaughter, and maybe it has something to do with my cooking and Irine's love for food.

five-minute chickpeas

- 1 Tbsp grapeseed oil
- 1 Tbsp fenugreek seeds
- ½ tsp asafoetida
- 1 cup finely chopped red onion
- 1 Tbsp finely chopped garlic
- 1 Tbsp Chana Masala (page 14)
- 1 tsp Garam Masala (page 12)
- ½ tsp salt
- 2 cups canned chickpeas, drained and washed with fresh water

Place the oil, fenugreek seeds, and asafoetida in a non-stick skillet over medium-high heat and cook for 10 seconds. Add the onion and garlic and cook for 2 minutes. Stir in the chana masala, garam masala, and salt and cook for 30 seconds. Add the chickpeas and cook for 1 minute.

Turn the heat off, put a lid on the pan, and let it sit for a few minutes before serving. Serve with brown rice or plain rotis (see page 20).

SERVES 4

Chickpeas take a long time to cook, so usually I make a big pot and freeze them. I soak them overnight in hot water and boil them the next day for an hour until I can crush them easily with a fork. I have used the canned chickpeas many times as well, and it doesn't change the flavour of the dish. If you use canned chickpeas, drain them, and rinse them with fresh water before adding them to the sauce.

my mother's chickpeas

- 2 Tbsp grapeseed oil
- 1 large onion, chopped
- 2 Tbsp finely chopped garlic
- 2 Tbsp finely chopped ginger
- 1 Tbsp cumin seeds
- ½ cup chopped fresh tomatoes
- 1 green chili, finely chopped (more for garnish)
- 2 tsp Chana Masala (page 14)
- 1 tsp salt
- 2 cups cooked chickpeas (or one 14 oz can)
- ¼ cup chopped fresh cilantro (optional)

Place the oil, onion, garlic, and ginger in a non-stick skillet over medium-high heat and cook for 3 minutes. Add the cumin seeds and cook for 1 minute. Stir in the tomatoes, green chili, chana masala, and salt. Reduce the heat to medium-low and cook for 5 minutes, stirring regularly.

Add the chickpeas to the skillet and cook for 1 minute. Turn the heat off, cover the pan with a lid, and let it sit for a few minutes before serving. Garnish with a sprinkle of cilantro or chopped green chili if desired. Serve with brown rice and Papaya Chicken (page 132).

SERVES 4

When I first came to Canada, I was very surprised to see that every single Indian dish was called curry. Where I grew up there was only one dish that was called curry, and this is it. This recipe is almost exactly the way my mother made potato curry. For the homemade buttermilk she used, I have substituted low-fat yogurt. This dish freezes very well.

traditional potato curry

2 Tbsp grapeseed oil
1 Tbsp cumin seeds
1 tsp fenugreek seeds
½ tsp asafoetida
2 onions, thinly sliced
2 Tbsp chopped garlic
2 Tbsp chopped ginger
2 large tomatoes, chopped
1 Tbsp Garam Masala (page 12)
1 tsp ground turmeric
1 tsp salt
2 cups low-fat plain yogurt
½ cup chickpea flour
2 cups water
2 large potatoes, thinly sliced

Place the oil, cumin seeds, fenugreek seeds, and asafoetida in a large non-stick skillet over medium-high heat and cook for 10 seconds. Add the onion, garlic, and ginger and cook for 3 minutes. Mix in the tomatoes, garam masala, turmeric, and salt. Cook for 1 minute, stirring regularly. Turn the heat to low.

Combine the yogurt, chickpea flour, and water in a large bowl. Whisk it together until the flour is completely mixed and there are no lumps. Add the yogurt mixture and the potatoes to the onion paste, turn the heat up, and bring the mixture to a boil. Cover the pot, reduce the heat to low and cook for 20 minutes. Serve over rice.

SERVES 4

Alloo matar *is the name for a dish that has green peas and potatoes. It was rarely made in my mother's kitchen—usually only for guests or sometimes for the men of the household. When I gained independence, for the first few months I made only those dishes that I couldn't have as a child. Then one day, as I was cooking, I realized how many people in my village still couldn't eat "privileged dishes" on a regular basis and I suddenly felt thankful. Inspired by that moment, I started giving cooking classes for charities and organizations that supported families, women, and children in need.*

green peas with paneer and potatoes

2 Tbsp grapeseed oil
1 large onion, finely chopped
2 Tbsp finely grated ginger
1 Tbsp finely grated garlic
1 Tbsp cumin seeds
1 Tbsp tomato paste
1 Tbsp Garam Masala (page 12)
1 tsp ground turmeric
1 tsp salt
4 large potatoes, peeled and finely chopped
1 cup crushed tomatoes
2 cups water
1 lb frozen peas

Place the oil, onion, ginger, and garlic in a non-stick skillet over medium-high heat and cook for 4 minutes. Add the cumin seeds and cook for 1 minute. Add the tomato paste and cook for 1 minute. Add the garam masala, turmeric, and salt, and cook for 2 minutes.

Stir in the potatoes, tomatoes, and water. Lower the heat to medium and cook until the potatoes are tender, 7 to 9 minutes. Add the peas and cook for 3 minutes. Serve with rice or plain rotis (see page 20).

NOTE For extra flavour, try adding 1 tsp finely chopped fenugreek leaves, 1 finely chopped medium green chili, and ¼ cup chopped fresh cilantro with the turmeric.

SERVES 4

I make these potatoes quite often on weekends in the mornings. As soon as the potatoes are cooked, I add four eggs and scramble them in the pan. We eat this along with brown toast and orange juice for a lovely brunch. My daughter always looks forward to it, and she thinks this is a perfect meal before her soccer game.

ginger potatoes

- 1 Tbsp grapeseed oil
- 2 Tbsp finely chopped ginger
- ¼ tsp salt
- 1 tsp fenugreek leaves
- ½ tsp red pepper flakes
- 1 lb small potatoes, boiled until they are almost cooked through, drained

Combine the oil, ginger, and salt in a non-stick pan over medium-high heat and cook for 1 minute. Stir in the fenugreek leaves and red pepper flakes and cook for 10 seconds. Add the potatoes and stir gently until the potatoes are completely coated with spices and cooked through, about 3 or 4 minutes.

Serve with Curried Turnips (page 114) and rice or plain rotis (page 20).

SERVES 4

It is interesting to see how different cultures prepare similar dishes. There are many stuffed pepper recipes in cookbooks using Mediterranean, Spanish, or other flavourings; here is my Indian version. Eileen Rawling, my recipe tester, gave this recipe five stars. Serve these with brown rice and Cauliflower with Yams (page 106).

stuffed green peppers

Step 1

- 4 potatoes, boiled and mashed
- 1 cup cooked brown rice
- 1 Tbsp Garam Masala (page 12)
- 1 Tbsp Chana Masala (page 14)
- 2 Tbsp grated ginger
- 1 green chili, chopped
- 1 tsp pomegranate powder
- 1 tsp salt
- 4 green, red, and/or yellow bell peppers

Place all the ingredients except the peppers in a bowl and mix them together gently.

Remove the stems and seeds from the green peppers. Fill the peppers with an equal amount of the potato mixture.

Step 2

- 2 Tbsp grapeseed oil
- 2 Tbsp grated garlic
- 1 tsp dried oregano
- 1 tsp salt
- 2 cups crushed tomatoes
- 1 cup red wine
- 1 cup water

Preheat the oven to 425°F.

Place the oil, garlic, oregano, and salt in a non-stick skillet over medium heat, and cook for 2 minutes. Add the crushed tomatoes, wine, and water, reduce the heat to low, and cook for 3 to 5 minutes.

Spread the sauce in a deep baking pan and place the filled peppers in the middle. Cover the pan with foil and bake for 25 minutes. Serve with the sauce spooned overtop.

SERVES 4

This recipe is similar to a traditional dish called **alloo gobi: alloo** *means "potatoes" and* **gobi** *means "cauliflower." I use yams because I love the flavour, but you can substitute potatoes if you prefer. I use this basic sauce for many other vegetarian recipes, such as zucchini and potatoes, green beans and potatoes, and eggplant and potatoes, but my favourite is shiitake mushrooms and green peas.*

cauliflower with yams

- 2 Tbsp grapeseed oil
- 1 large onion, finely chopped
- 1 Tbsp grated ginger
- 1 Tbsp cumin seeds
- 1 Tbsp Garam Masala (page 12)
- 1 tsp ground turmeric
- 1 tsp salt
- 2 medium-sized ripe tomatoes, finely chopped
- 2 large yams, finely chopped
- ½ cup water
- 1 large cauliflower, chopped into bite-sized pieces

Place the oil and onion in a non-stick skillet over medium-high heat and cook for 4 minutes. Add the ginger, cumin seeds, garam masala, turmeric, and salt and cook for 2 minutes. Stir in the tomatoes, yams, and water, cover the pan with a lid, and reduce the heat to medium-low. Cook until the yams are tender, about 7 minutes, stirring occasionally.

Add the cauliflower, stirring to mix everything well. Put the lid back on, and cook until the cauliflower is still somewhat crunchy, 5 to 8 minutes. Enjoy with rice or plain rotis (see page 20).

NOTE I always use organic cauliflower because of its superior flavour. I like my cauliflower very crunchy—and not overcooking it helps retain nutrients.

SERVES 4

Sabji *means "vegetable dish." When my father came home from work at the end of the day, he always asked as he entered the door, "What sabji is made today?" When I tell my daughter that sabji was made every day in my mother's kitchen, she wonders how people in the village lived eating sabji so often. It's hard for her to understand that when food is scarce and there are not too many options, one becomes thankful for whatever food is available.*

everyday stir-fry (sabji)

- 2 Tbsp grapeseed oil
- 1 onion, chopped
- 2 Tbsp finely grated ginger
- ½ cup chopped tomatoes
- 1 green chili, finely chopped
- 1 Tbsp Garam Masala (page 12)
- 1 tsp salt
- 1 lb green beans, chopped
- 1 lb Chinese cabbage, chopped in bigger chunks

Place the oil, onion, and ginger in a wok or a non-stick skillet over medium-high heat and cook for 4 minutes. Add the tomatoes, green chili, garam masala, and salt, and cook for 3 minutes. Add the green beans, reduce the heat to medium, and cook until the beans are tender, about 3 minutes, stirring regularly. Add the Chinese cabbage and cook for 2 minutes.

Turn the heat off, cover with a lid, and let it sit for a few minutes. Serve over rice or noodles.

NOTE To add nutrients and crunch, sprinkle 1 Tbsp of flaxseed overtop before serving. For a meat stir-fry, add 1 lb diced boneless chicken breast with the tomatoes; return to a simmer and continue with the recipe.

SERVES 4

I thought at first I'd use this recipe as an appetizer—cooking all the spices with paneer, sprinkling the paneer on top of individual slices of zucchini, and baking it. I changed my mind because the flavours go very well with rice and it also makes a tasty filling for lunch wraps.

zucchini paneer

2 Tbsp grapeseed oil
1 Tbsp fenugreek seeds
1 Tbsp cumin seeds
1 large red onion, chopped
2 Tbsp grated ginger
1 lb zucchini, cubed
1 cup chopped tomatoes
1 tsp ground turmeric
1 tsp red pepper flakes
1 tsp salt
1 cup cubed Homemade Paneer (page 41), pan-fried
1 Tbsp Garam Masala (page 12)
¼ cup chopped fresh cilantro

Place the oil, fenugreek seeds, and cumin seeds in a non-stick skillet over medium heat and cook for 10 seconds. Add the onion and ginger and cook over medium-high heat for 4 minutes. Stir in the zucchini, tomatoes, turmeric, red pepper flakes, and salt. Cook on medium heat until the zucchini is tender, about 10 minutes.

Stir in the paneer and turn the heat off. Sprinkle the garam masala and cilantro overtop, cover with a lid, and let sit for 10 minutes before serving.

Serve over rice or plain rotis (see page 20). Enjoy!

SERVES 4

When I first found out my son had food allergies, I spent a lot of time researching the health benefits of vegetables. Broccoli showed up over and over as being rich in a number of nutrients. A relative of cauliflower not used in Indian cuisine, it is delicious in this simple preparation with garlic and garam masala.

broccoli masala

- 1 lb broccoli, cut into small pieces
- 1 tsp grapeseed oil
- 1 tsp grated garlic
- 1 tsp Garam Masala (page 12)
- ½ tsp salt

Steam the broccoli until the crunchy side of tender. Place the oil and garlic in a non-stick skillet over medium-high heat and cook for 1 minute. Add the garam masala and salt and cook for 10 seconds. Add the broccoli and cook for 20 seconds, mixing gently until the masala is evenly distributed. Serve on top of rice or as a side dish with Halibut Masala (page 139).

SERVES 4

White radish is called **mooli** *in Punjabi. You can buy it in many supermarkets as well as at ethnic markets, sometimes sold as "daikon." We grew it in our vegetable garden and used it raw in salads and also cooked with spices and herbs. This dish takes just a few minutes to make. I use the leftovers and brown rice to make lunch wraps.*

spiced white indian radish

- 2 Tbsp grapeseed oil
- 2 Tbsp grated ginger
- 1 Tbsp Garam Masala (page 12)
- 1 tsp ground turmeric
- 1 tsp salt
- 1 lb white radish, grated
- ¼ cup low-fat sour cream

Combine the oil and ginger in a non-stick skillet over medium-high heat and cook until the ginger is golden brown, about 2 to 3 minutes. Add the garam masala, turmeric, and salt and cook for 1 minute. Stir in the radish and cook on medium heat for 3 to 5 minutes.

Turn the heat off and gently mix in the sour cream. Serve on top of rice or with plain rotis (see page 20). Enjoy!

SERVES 4

In my village we grew two different types of turnip: yellow and green. My favourites were the green ones, which were soft as zucchini and would melt in your mouth. I can still taste the tomato sauce when my mother made this dish, called **teendai**. *Sometimes she cut the turnips in half, filled them with garam masala, and let them toast for hours before she added them to the onion/tomato paste. As we didn't cook rice very often, we had rotis with this dish.*

curried turnips

2 Tbsp grapeseed oil
2 Tbsp grated ginger
1 Tbsp Garam Masala (page 12)
1 tsp fenugreek seeds
1 tsp ground turmeric
1 tsp salt
2 tomatoes, chopped
1 lb turnips, chopped into 1-inch pieces
1 cup water

Place the oil and ginger in a large non-stick skillet and cook over medium-high heat for 2 minutes. Add the garam masala, fenugreek seeds, turmeric, and salt, and cook for 1 minute. Stir in the tomatoes and cook for 2 minutes. Add the turnips and water, and bring to a boil. Reduce the heat to a simmer and cook for 13 to 15 minutes.

Serve with rice or plain rotis (see page 20).

SERVES 4

Roasted eggplants are absolutely the best. My mom would place them on the coals in the barbecue pit, where they would roast for hours on very low heat. Now I can throw them in the oven for an hour, and voilà!

baked eggplant with paneer

4 eggplant
2 Tbsp grapeseed oil
1 large onion, chopped
2 Tbsp grated ginger
2 cups cubed tomatoes
1 green chili, finely chopped
1 Tbsp Garam Masala (page 12)
1 tsp ground turmeric
1 tsp salt
1 cup cubed Homemade Paneer (page 41), pan-fried

Preheat the oven to 350°F. Place the eggplants on a baking sheet and bake for 1 hour. Peel off the skin and mash the eggplant gently with a fork.

Place the oil, onion, and ginger in a non-stick skillet over medium-high heat and cook for 5 minutes. Add the tomatoes, green chili, garam masala, turmeric, and salt, and cook over medium-low heat for 5 minutes. Gently mix in the eggplant, reduce the heat to very low, and cook for 1 minute.

Mix in the paneer, cover the dish, and let it sit for 5 minutes before serving.

SERVES 4

Over the last eight years, I have met many people in my cooking classes who don't like eggplant. It seems to be one of those vegetables that people either love or hate. This recipe is dedicated to risk takers, to those who do not want to have anything to do with the vegetable but are still willing to experience the way mango blends with the spices and the unique flavour and texture of eggplant. For this recipe, it doesn't matter what kind of eggplant you purchase. Experiment and have fun with it. Just remember, it won't bite you back.

eggplant with mango sauce

- 2 Tbsp grapeseed oil
- 1 red onion, finely chopped
- 1 Tbsp grated ginger
- 1 Tbsp tomato paste
- 1 tsp cumin seeds
- 1 tomato, finely chopped
- 1 green chili, finely chopped
- 1 tsp Garam Masala (page 12)
- 1 tsp ground turmeric
- 1 tsp salt
- 1 medium-sized eggplant, chopped into 1-inch pieces
- ½ cup water
- ¾ cup fresh mango pulp (about 1 medium-sized ripe mango)

Place the oil, onion, and ginger in a non-stick skillet and cook over medium-high heat for 4 minutes. Add the tomato paste and cumin seeds and cook for 1 minute. Add the tomato, chili, garam masala, turmeric, and salt, and cook for 2 minutes.

Reduce the heat to medium, add the eggplant and water, and cook until the eggplant is tender, 12 to 15 minutes. Add the mango pulp and cook for 1 more minute, stirring gently. Turn the heat off and cover the pan with a lid for 5 minutes before serving. Serve with rice or plain rotis (see page 20).

NOTE If fresh mango is not available, canned mango will do the trick; mash the mango with a fork before adding it to the eggplant mixture.

SERVES 4

In the village, rice was usually reserved for special occasions, such as weddings or events that celebrated the birth of a boy. When my mother cooked this dish, I would smell the basmati rice from the backyard and know she was in a good mood or a guest was arriving!

brown rice with toasted cumin and green peas

- 2 Tbsp grapeseed oil
- 1 red onion, finely chopped
- 1 tsp cumin seeds
- 1 tsp curry leaves
- 1 tsp Garam Masala (page 12)
- 1 tsp salt
- 1 cup frozen peas
- 4 cups cooked brown basmati rice

Place the oil and onion in a non-stick skillet over medium-high heat and cook for 4 minutes. Add the cumin, curry leaves, garam masala, and salt, and cook for 2 minutes. Stir in the frozen peas and cook until the peas are tender, 3 to 5 minutes. Add the rice and mix everything gently until the spices are evenly distributed. Enjoy!

NOTE To vary this dish, use fava beans instead of peas.

SERVES 4

Not only is asparagus a great source of several nutrients, it is also very quick to cook. This can be ready in ten minutes, including prep time!

punjabi asparagus

2 Tbsp grapeseed oil
1 Tbsp chopped garlic
1 tsp fenugreek seeds
1 tsp cumin seeds
1 tsp Garam Masala (page 12)
¼ tsp salt
1 lb asparagus, tough ends trimmed off

Place the oil, garlic, fenugreek seeds, and cumin seeds in a non-stick skillet and cook over medium-high heat for 30 seconds. Add the garam masala and salt, and cook for 1 minute, stirring constantly. Add the asparagus and cook over medium-low heat until tender, 3 to 5 minutes.

Serve on top of any pasta or rice.

NOTE Nuts have many health benefits, and toasted almonds are a tasty addition to this dish.

SERVES 4

It is a little tricky to make this dish. You must use absolutely no water, and it needs to be completely cooked or it will have a greasy, slimy, watery texture. Usually 10 to 12 minutes on medium heat will make a perfect okra dish. Take the risk and experiment with this vegetable if you've never tried it before.

okra with pan-fried paneer

- 2 Tbsp grapeseed oil
- 1 large red onion, chopped
- 1 Tbsp grated ginger
- 1 tsp ground turmeric
- 1 tsp salt
- ½ cup cherry tomatoes, halved
- 1 lb okra, washed and cut in bite-sized pieces
- 1 cup bite-sized pieces of Homemade Paneer (page 41), pan-fried
- 1 tsp Garam Masala (page 12)

Place the oil and onion in a non-stick skillet over medium-high heat and cook for 4 minutes, stirring regularly. Add the ginger, turmeric, and salt, and cook for 1 minute. Reduce the heat to medium, add the tomato, and cook for 2 minutes. Stir in the okra and cook until it's tender, about 12 minutes.

Stir the paneer into the sauce and sprinkle the garam masala over the dish (do not mix in the garam masala yet). Turn off the heat and cover the pot with a lid.

Let sit for 10 minutes, mix everything well, and serve.

SERVES 4

When I made this for the first time at a cooking class, I mentioned that I hadn't cooked the dish before but knew exactly what it would taste like. As I mixed a little bit of this and a little of that, someone took notes and emailed the recipe to me for this book. This is a very elegant company dish.

mushrooms with wine and low-fat cream cheese

- 2 Tbsp grapeseed oil
- 1 tsp asafoetida
- 1 tsp mustard seeds
- 1 Tbsp grated garlic
- 1 tsp Garam Masala (page 12)
- 1 tsp Chana Masala (page 14)
- ½ tsp salt
- ¼ cup red wine (Merlot)
- 2 Tbsp low-fat cream cheese
- 1 cup sliced shiitake mushrooms
- 1 cup sliced portobello mushrooms

Place the oil, asafoetida, and mustard seeds in a non-stick pan over medium-high heat and cook for 10 seconds. Add the garlic, garam masala, chana masala, and salt, and cook for 1 minute. Stir in the wine and cream cheese, reduce the heat to medium-low, and cook for 1 minute. Add the mushrooms and cook until they are tender, 3 to 5 minutes. Serve over rice.

SERVES 4

A few years ago I started experimenting with South Indian spices such as mustard seeds, curry leaves, and sambar powder. This was around the time I met my friend Kathy, a retired nurse, who told me she had never tried Indian food. I invited her over for lunch and made this, and after that she couldn't get enough of Indian food. She told me she couldn't find the same flavours at any restaurant and finally asked me for this recipe. This is dedicated to Kathy and Bill, who last year became my adopted parents.

south indian mushrooms

- 2 Tbsp grapeseed oil
- 1 Tbsp brown mustard seeds
- 1 tsp asafoetida
- 2 Tbsp grated ginger
- 2 Tbsp grated garlic
- ½ cup chopped green onions
- ¼ cup dried curry leaves
- ¼ cup toasted cashews (optional)
- 1 Tbsp Sambar Powder (page 17)
- 1 tsp red chili powder
- ½ tsp ground turmeric
- 2 cups chopped portobello mushrooms
- 1 cup chopped shiitake mushrooms
- ½ cup low-fat coconut milk

Place the oil, mustard seeds, and asafoetida in a non-stick skillet over medium-high heat and cook for 10 seconds. Add the ginger and garlic and cook for 2 minutes. Stir in the green onions, curry leaves, cashews, sambar powder, chili powder, and turmeric, and cook for 2 minutes.

Add the mushrooms and coconut milk, place a lid on the pot, and cook over medium-low heat until the mushrooms are tender, 5 to 7 minutes.

Serve with Buffalo Masala (page 158) and plain rotis (see page 20).

SERVES 4

It's great to live in a multicultural society where spices from all over the world are easily available. When I first smelled fresh oregano and basil at a farmers' market, I knew I had to use these herbs in my cooking. This fusion recipe has the aroma and flavours of both an Indian and an Italian kitchen.

curried spaghetti sauce

2 Tbsp grapeseed oil
¼ cup dried curry leaves
1 Tbsp mustard seeds
2 Tbsp grated garlic
2 Tbsp tomato paste
1 Tbsp ground cumin
1 Tbsp ground coriander
1 tsp dried oregano
1 tsp dried basil
1 tsp salt
2 cups crushed tomatoes (one 14 oz can)
¼ cup red wine
½ cup water

Place the oil, curry leaves, and mustard seeds in a non-stick skillet over medium heat, and cook for 10 seconds. Add the garlic, tomato paste, cumin, coriander, oregano, basil, and salt, and cook for 2 minutes.

Stir in the tomatoes, wine, and water. Reduce the heat to medium-low, and cook for 15 minutes.

Serve over spaghetti.

NOTE For a non-vegetarian dish, add ground buffalo meat after the curry leaves; cook the meat for 3 minutes before adding the rest of the ingredients.

SERVES 4

chicken, seafood, and meat dishes

Growing up vegetarian, I had never eaten butter chicken. The first time I tried it was in a restaurant here in Canada, and I could see why people loved it—chicken cooked with cream and ghee (Indian butter)—but I was turned off by the heaviness of the sauce. It inspired me to create my own healthy version of this popular Indian dish. My 14-year-old daughter cannot get enough of this, and every time her friends stay over, they request my no-butter chicken.

bal's no-butter chicken

- ¼ cup grapeseed oil
- 2 large onions, chopped
- 2 Tbsp finely chopped garlic
- 2 Tbsp finely chopped ginger
- 2 Tbsp tomato paste
- 1 Tbsp cumin seeds
- 1 Tbsp Garam Masala (page 12)
- 1 Tbsp brown sugar
- 1 tsp red pepper flakes
- 1 tsp ground turmeric
- 1 tsp salt
- 1 lb boneless, skinless chicken breast, cut into bite-sized pieces
- ¾ cup low-fat plain yogurt
- ¼ cup water

Place the oil in a non-stick skillet over high heat, add the onions, and sauté until dark golden brown. Add the garlic and ginger, reduce the heat to medium, and cook for 2 minutes. Add the tomato paste and cumin seeds and cook for 30 seconds.

Reduce the heat to low, add the garam masala, brown sugar, red pepper flakes, turmeric, and salt, and cook for 2 minutes. Mix in the chicken and cook until the chicken is almost done, about 5 to 7 minutes. Add the yogurt and water, and cook until the chicken is fully cooked, about 5 minutes. Serve it with brown rice or plain rotis (see page 20).

NOTE Feel free to use whipping cream instead of yogurt. Even I give in and indulge from time to time!

SUGGESTED WINE Gewürztraminer

SERVES 4

I grew up in a vegetarian home. Maybe once or twice in my life in the village, I sneaked a taste of chicken sauce during a wedding. After a few tries, I have created the exact taste of the chicken sauce I remember from when I was a little girl. Please try it, experiment with the spices, and feel free to send me your feedback!

traditional chicken

2 Tbsp grapeseed oil
1 large onion, finely chopped
2 Tbsp finely chopped garlic
2 Tbsp finely chopped ginger
1 Tbsp cumin seeds
1 tsp fenugreek seeds
1 Tbsp tomato paste
1 Tbsp Garam Masala (page 12)
1 green chili, finely chopped
1 tsp Spanish paprika
1 tsp turmeric
1 tsp salt
1 lb bone-in chicken thighs
2 cups chopped tomatoes
2 cups finely chopped potatoes
½ cup loosely packed chopped fresh cilantro
3 cups water

Combine the oil, onion, garlic, and ginger in a non-stick skillet over medium-high heat, and cook for 5 minutes. Add the cumin and fenugreek seeds and cook for 10 seconds. Add the tomato paste, garam masala, chili, paprika, turmeric, and salt, and cook for 2 minutes, stirring frequently. Add the chicken and cook for 4 minutes, turning the chicken frequently. Add the tomatoes, potatoes, cilantro, and water; mix everything well, and bring the dish to a boil.

Reduce the heat to a simmer, put a lid on the pot, and cook for 15 minutes or until the chicken is cooked through. Serve with rice or plain rotis (see page 20).

NOTE For another flavour, add 1 Tbsp dried curry leaves and 1 Tbsp fenugreek leaves along with the spices.

SERVES 4

Brad's cousin Jordan is 15 years old. The first time I met him, when he was six years old, he told me how much he loved Indian food. Right away I adopted him as one of my favourite nephews. Last year I went to visit him, and he asked me if I could make him some Indian food. I went through his fridge and spice cabinet and made this dish.

fusion peach chicken for jordan

- 1 cup regular spaghetti sauce
- 1 cup peach yogurt
- 2 Tbsp tandoori paste
- 1 Tbsp Garam Masala (page 12)
- 1 tsp garlic powder
- 1 tsp ground dried ginger
- 1 tsp red chili flakes
- 1 tsp salt
- 1 cup water
- 1 lb boneless, skinless chicken breast, cut into bite-sized pieces

Preheat the oven to 375°F. Combine all the ingredients in a deep baking dish and mix well. Place the dish in the oven and cover with foil. Bake for 25 minutes. Remove the foil and bake for 5 to 8 more minutes. Serve over rice.

NOTE Tandoori paste is available in most supermarkets and in Indian grocery stores.

SERVES 4

I never had the opportunity to travel within India, so I had South Indian food for the first time in Canada. I instantly fell in love with the flavourings, which include mustard seeds, asafoetida, curry leaves, and coconut milk. This was one of the first dishes I created.

chicken south indian style

2 Tbsp grapeseed oil
1 onion, chopped
2 Tbsp grated ginger
2 Tbsp grated garlic
¼ cup curry leaves
1 Tbsp brown mustard seeds
1 Tbsp Sambar Powder (page 17)
1 tsp asafoetida
1 tsp red chili powder
½ tsp ground turmeric
2 lb boneless, skinless chicken breast, cut into bite-sized pieces
2 cups chopped tomatoes
1 cup low-fat coconut milk
½ cup water

Place the oil, onion, ginger, and garlic in a non-stick skillet over medium-high heat and cook for 4 minutes, stirring regularly. Add the curry leaves, mustard seeds, sambar powder, asafoetida, chili powder, and turmeric, and cook for 2 minutes. Add the chicken and cook for 3 minutes. Stir in the tomatoes and cook for 2 minutes. Add the coconut milk and water and cook until the chicken is tender, 3 to 5 minutes. Serve with rice.

NOTE For a delicious nutty flavour, cook ¼ cup raw cashews with the sauce.

SUGGESTED WINE unoaked Chardonnay or French Chablis

SERVES 4

This dish can be whipped up in minutes if the curry paste is already prepared—a great reason to have it on hand in the refrigerator or freezer!

indian-thai fusion prawns

2 Tbsp grapeseed oil
4 Tbsp Fusion Curry Paste (page 15)
20 uncooked prawns, peeled

Place the oil and curry paste in a non-stick pan over medium heat and cook for 1 minute. Add the prawns and cook through, about 5 minutes. Serve over rice.

NOTE For a rich, creamy coconut flavour, add ¼ cup of low-fat coconut milk when the prawns are almost cooked, and continue to cook until prawns are completely done. Or for those who don't like seafood, replace the prawns with 1 lb cubed boneless, skinless chicken breast. For a vegetarian version, substitute 2 cups (about 1 lb) chopped green beans.

SUGGESTED WINE Sauvignon Blanc

SERVES 4

The first time I tried halibut was in a fancy French restaurant. The fish just melted in my mouth and, of course, the butter made it very yummy. Since I am not used to eating butter, I paid a big price the next day. I wanted to create my own recipe for halibut that was quick, healthy, and just as delicious. The peach sauce and garam masala make an aromatic and flavourful dish.

halibut with peach sauce

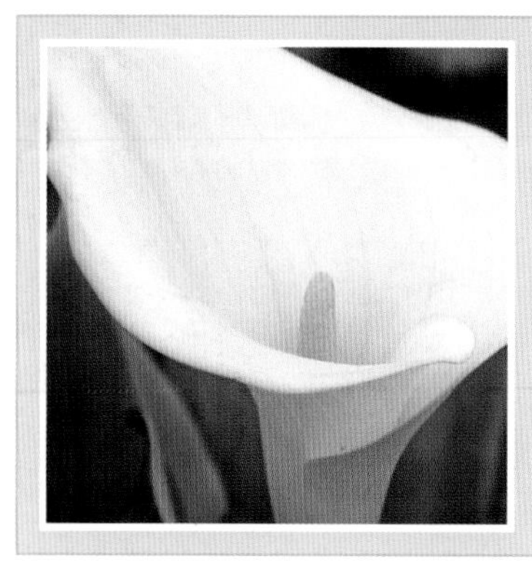

- 4 fresh halibut steaks, each about 6–8 oz
- 1 Tbsp grapeseed oil
- 1 tsp asafoetida
- 1 tsp fenugreek seeds
- 1 Tbsp finely chopped garlic
- 1 Tbsp Garam Masala (page 12)
- 1 Tbsp Chana Masala (page 14)
- 1 Tbsp tomato paste
- 1 Tbsp finely chopped medium-hot green chili
- 1 tsp salt
- 1 cup canned peaches, chopped
- ¼ cup peach syrup

Preheat the barbecue to medium-high. Place the steaks on the grill and cook for about 8 minutes, turning once. When cooked, the flakes should separate easily with a fork.

While the halibut is cooking, make the sauce. Place the oil, asafoetida, and fenugreek seeds in a non-stick skillet over medium-high heat and cook for 5 seconds. Stir in the garlic, garam masala, chana masala, tomato paste, green chili, and salt. Reduce the heat to medium and cook for 2 minutes. Add the peaches and syrup, reduce the heat to low, and simmer for 3 to 5 minutes.

Pour the sauce over the halibut before serving. This dish is great with rice and Cauliflower with Yams (page 106).

NOTE Instead of grilling the halibut, you can broil the steaks in the oven for 7 to 10 minutes.

SUGGESTED WINE Viognier

SERVES 4

The caste system was still present in various parts of India, particularly rural areas, when I grew up. The upper castes had access to different kinds of food, and to education, medical care, and a luxurious lifestyle, and for the lower castes it was the totally opposite. In my village we were not even allowed to be friends with the lower caste, but I secretly developed a friendship with a lovely girl named Keepan. When we met we exchanged food. Only lower caste people ate fish, so she brought me fish, and I brought her dairy products made with bison milk. I thought the fish Keepan brought me was the best food I had ever eaten. Now I wonder if I loved the fish because of the coriander and asafoetida or because it was prohibited! I might never have the answer, but those who try this recipe tell me they want to lick their plates after eating it. You be the judge.

halibut masala

2 Tbsp grapeseed oil
1 tsp fenugreek seeds
½ tsp asafoetida
2 Tbsp curry leaves
1 Tbsp grated ginger
1 Tbsp grated garlic
1 tsp ground coriander
1 tsp ground cumin
1 Tbsp tomato paste
1 green chili, finely chopped
1 tsp brown sugar
1 tsp salt
¼ cup low-fat plain yogurt
¼ cup water
4 fresh halibut steaks, each about 6–8 oz

Preheat the oven to 350°F. Combine the oil, fenugreek seeds, and asafoetida in a non-stick pan over medium-high heat and cook for 10 seconds. Mix in the curry leaves, ginger, garlic, coriander, and cumin, and cook for 2 minutes. Stir in the tomato paste, chili, brown sugar, and salt, and cook for 2 minutes. Add the yogurt and water and stir until completely combined.

Place the fish in a baking pan that will fit it nicely. Pour the sauce over the fish, and cover the pan with foil. Bake in the preheated oven until the halibut is cooked through, about 20 minutes. Serve over rice.

SUGGESTED WINE Chenin Blanc

SERVES 4

When I first started going out with Brad, cod was the first meal he made for me. I was very impressed with the perfectly done cod, green peas, and brown rice. Then he invited me for dinner again, and I was a little surprised that he made the same dish, although it sort of made sense because he knew how much I had loved it the first time. When I was invited for dinner a third time, a thought went through my mind—could it be another cod night? It turned out it was! I finally put two and two together: he was not a risk taker and liked to stick to what he did best. This dish is quick, delicious, healthy, and easy to make.

grilled cod and asparagus with mint chutney

- 4 cod fillets, each about 6 oz
- 1 Tbsp grapeseed oil
- 1 lb asparagus, steamed
- Mint Chutney (page 35)
- salt and freshly ground pepper

Preheat the barbecue to 400°F. Brush the cod fillets with grapeseed oil. Reduce the heat to 375°F and place the fish on the grill. Cook for 3 to 4 minutes on each side, until the cod flakes with gentle pressure.

Place asparagus on each plate and top with the cod. Season with salt and pepper, and serve with chutney. For a nice presentation, garnish with lemon zest and fennel seeds if you'd like.

SUGGESTED WINE Serve this dish with a dry, crisp white wine. I like the Mission Hill Family Estate Reserve Sauvignon Blanc.

SERVES 4

Salmon is a very forgiving fish. You can bake it, grill it, pan-fry it, or barbecue it, as long as you do not overcook it. Salmon is full of nutrients and healthy fats, and this combination with mango salsa makes a gourmet dish.

grilled sockeye salmon with mango salsa

Salsa

- ½ mango, finely chopped
- 2 Tbsp mango juice
- 1 Tbsp finely chopped fresh cilantro
- 1 Tbsp finely chopped red onion
- 1 Tbsp lemon juice
- ½ tsp fennel seeds
- ¼ tsp salt

Mix all the ingredients and let sit for 5 minutes while you grill the fish.

Salmon

- 2 lb salmon fillet
- 1 Tbsp olive oil
- 1 tsp Sambar Powder (page 17)
- ½ tsp Garam Masala (page 12)
- ¼ tsp salt

Gently rub the salmon fillet with oil and season with the sambar powder, garam masala, and salt. Preheat the barbecue to medium-high and place the salmon skin down on the grill. Cook for about 12 minutes, until the fish flakes with gentle pressure from a fork.

To serve, place a piece of salmon on each plate and top with a spoonful of mango salsa. Serve with Broccoli Masala (page 110) and brown basmati rice.

SUGGESTED WINE Pinot Noir

SERVES 4

Our son, Aaron, has allergies to fish, so I don't cook it very often at home. But here is a funny story about fish. When we went to the allergy specialist, the doctor told us the best way to find out if Aaron had grown out of his allergies was to rub some fish on his arm. My husband took that suggestion very seriously. Last summer when we went to the Kootenays for our summer holidays, the first thing Brad did when he came back from fishing was rub fish on Aaron's arm. A few tourists observed Brad doing this and asked me if that was a tradition from my village.

salmon cooked with traditional curry

- one 2 lb coho salmon
- 2 Tbsp grapeseed oil
- 1 Tbsp fenugreek seeds
- 1 Tbsp cumin seeds
- 2 Tbsp chopped garlic
- 2 Tbsp chopped ginger
- 1 medium green chili, finely chopped
- 1 Tbsp tomato paste
- 1 Tbsp Garam Masala (page 12)
- 1 tsp ground turmeric
- 1 tsp salt
- 2 Tbsp chickpea flour
- 3 cups water
- 1 cup low-fat plain yogurt
- 1 cup crushed tomatoes

Spray a baking pan lightly with cooking spray. Place the salmon in the pan, and broil it in the oven (on the top rack) for 12 to 14 minutes, without turning, until the fish is browned and flakes with gentle pressure from a fork.

While the fish is cooking, combine the oil, fenugreek and cumin seeds in a non-stick skillet over medium-high heat and cook for 10 seconds. Mix in the garlic, ginger, and green chili and cook for 1 minute. Stir in the tomato paste, garam masala, turmeric, and salt. Reduce the heat to medium and cook for 2 minutes, continuing to stir.

In a separate bowl combine the chickpea flour and water using a whisk to ensure it is well mixed. Add the chickpea mixture, the yogurt, and the crushed tomatoes to the sauce. Bring to a boil, turn the heat to low, and simmer for 10 minutes.

Gently cut the salmon into 2-inch squares. Place the salmon pieces in the sauce, turn the heat off, and cover the pan with a lid. Let it sit for 5 minutes before serving. Serve on top of rice or with naan (page 23) or plain rotis (page 20).

SUGGESTED WINE Rosé or Riesling

SERVES 4

When a newspaper reporter came to interview me, she asked what my indulgences were. I told her: a glass of fine red wine, some milk chocolate, a good piece of lamb, and a fishnet necklace from Tiffany's. She laughed hard and literally fell off the chair. This dish falls into the category of indulgences, and I cook it only once a month. Would I call this dish quick and healthy? Maybe not! But it fills my heart with pleasure and my house with beautiful aromas.

once-a-month lamb

- 1½ lb boneless lamb stew meat (preferably shoulder)
- ¼ cup whole wheat flour
- 1 Tbsp coriander seeds, partly ground
- 1 tsp Chana Masala (page 14)
- 2 Tbsp grapeseed oil
- 1 red onion, chopped
- 2 Tbsp grated garlic
- 2 Tbsp grated ginger
- 1 Tbsp cumin seeds
- 1 Tbsp Garam Masala (page 12)
- 1 Tbsp tomato paste
- 1 green chili, finely chopped
- ¼ cup chocolate chips
- 2 cups chopped tomatoes
- 1 cup chopped red bell pepper
- 1 cup red wine
- 1 tsp salt
- 2 cups water

Trim the lamb of the excess fat and cut into 2-inch cubes. Mix together the flour, coriander seeds, and chana masala in a bowl. Transfer the mixture onto a plate and lightly coat the lamb.

Heat the oil in a non-stick skillet over medium heat, add the lamb and brown on all sides. Drain off all the fat and add the onion, garlic, ginger, and cumin seeds, and cook on medium heat for 2 minutes, stirring frequently. Add the garam masala, tomato paste, green chili, and chocolate chips, and cook for 1 minute, stirring constantly. Add the tomatoes, bell pepper, wine, salt, and water, and cook for 10 more minutes.

Transfer the mixture to a slow cooker, and cook on the low setting for 10 hours or on high for 5 hours.

NOTE For a healthier dish, replace the lamb with buffalo meat, use sugar-free chocolate instead of regular chocolate chips, and substitute vegetable stock for the wine.

SUGGESTED WINE Bordeaux or Cabernet Sauvignon

SERVES 4

Ten years ago, I met my friend Michèle through Brad. Michèle has a fine palate because she has travelled all over the world for marathons and Ironman events. When I wanted to test some recipes, I called her and asked if she could be the taster. Michèle is very picky when it comes to food, so I knew it would be challenging to please her. This is one of the recipes she tasted. The combination of black cherries and fennel seeds gives a great aroma to this elegant dish. Serve with rice and Broccoli Masala (page 110).

lamb with black cherry sauce

Lamb

1 Tbsp grapeseed oil
2 lb rack of lamb

Rub

2 tsp ground cumin
2 tsp Garam Masala (page 12)
1 tsp fennel seeds
¼ tsp ground cinnamon
¼ tsp salt
¼ tsp pepper

Combine all the rub ingredients in a bowl and rub the mixture over all the surface of the lamb. Heat the oil in a heavy-bottomed skillet over medium-high heat. Place seasoned lamb in the skillet and brown on all sides, about 3 to 4 minutes.

Preheat the oven to 450°F. Place the lamb on a baking sheet and bake for 15 to 17 minutes. Remove from the oven and let sit for 5 minutes.

Continues on page 150

Lamb with Black Cherry Sauce continued

Sauce

1 Tbsp grapeseed oil
½ tsp asafoetida
2 Tbsp chopped garlic
1 tsp fenugreek seeds
2 tsp Garam Masala (page 12)
¼ tsp ground cardamom
one 14 oz can pitted cherries and juice

While the lamb is baking, prepare the sauce. Place the oil and asafoetida in a saucepan and cook for 5 seconds over medium-high heat. Mix in the garlic and fenugreek seeds and cook for 1 minute. Stir in the garam masala and cardamom. Cook for 10 seconds, and then add the cherries, including the juice. Reduce the heat to low and simmer the sauce for 7 to 9 minutes.

Remove the sauce from the heat and process it using a food processor to thicken the sauce. Pour some sauce on a serving platter, place the lamb on top, and then pour the rest over the lamb.

SUGGESTED WINE New World Merlot

SERVES 4

With this recipe I was originally thinking of lamb. When a devoted student (now dear friend), Cheryl, offered her kitchen to test some of my recipes, I didn't know she didn't eat lamb—suprising because she ate every other meat. She said she just felt sorry for the lamb. I told her that if I suddenly felt the same way, the dish wouldn't turn out because it would be made with guilt, not love. So we decided to use pork instead. When I finished making the sauce, the kitchen was filled with the most beautiful aromas. Raspberries can sometimes be intrusive, but here they are a perfect complement.

pork tenderloin with raspberry sauce

2 lb pork tenderloin
1 Tbsp grapeseed oil
1 tsp asafoetida
1 tsp ground cardamom
1 Tbsp finely chopped garlic
1 Tbsp finely chopped ginger
1 medium-sized green chili, finely chopped
1 Tbsp tomato paste
1 Tbsp Garam Masala (page 12)
1 tsp ground turmeric
1 tsp salt
1 cup frozen raspberries
¼ cup crushed tomatoes
1 Tbsp brown sugar
1 cup water

Preheat the barbecue to medium-high. Gently place the tenderloin on the grill and close the lid. Cook for 17 to 20 minutes, turning once. To test for doneness, pierce the pork; the juices should run clear. Also, if you cut the pork, you should see just a bit of pink remaining inside. Place the meat on the cutting board and tent with foil. Let it sit for 10 minutes.

While the pork is grilling, combine the oil, asafoetida, and ground cardamom in a non-stick pan over medium-high heat and cook for 5 seconds. Add the garlic, ginger, and chili, and cook for 1 minute. Stir in the tomato paste, garam masala, turmeric, and salt, and cook on medium heat for 1 minute, continuing to stir. Add the raspberries, crushed tomatoes, sugar, and water. Simmer the sauce for 10 to 15 minutes, stirring frequently.

Place the pork on a platter and pour the sauce on top. Serve with rice and plain rotis (see page 20).

SERVES 4

This is a very quick and yummy recipe. When you're pressed for time, just use frozen precooked meatballs, which can be purchased from the freezer section of any supermarket. Serve these over rice.

curried meatballs

Meatballs

1 lb ground meat (or use a combination of ground beef, veal, and pork)
2 eggs
⅓ cup breadcrumbs
¼ cup grated Parmesan cheese
1 Tbsp fennel seeds
1 Tbsp cumin seeds
1 tsp crushed coriander seeds
1 tsp salt
3 Tbsp grapeseed oil

Sauce

2 Tbsp grapeseed oil
1 large onion, chopped
2 Tbsp finely chopped ginger
2 Tbsp finely chopped garlic
1 Tbsp cumin seeds
2 Tbsp tomato paste
1 green chili, finely chopped
1 Tbsp Garam Masala (see page 12)
1 Tbsp fenugreek leaves
1 tsp ground turmeric
2 tsp salt
2 cups crushed tomatoes
1 lb frozen spinach, partly thawed and chopped
3 cups water

Place all the meatball ingredients, except for the oil, in a bowl. Combine well with your hands and form the meat into 2-inch balls. Add the oil to a non-stick pan over medium-high, add the meatballs, and brown on all sides. Reduce the heat to low and cook until the meat is cooked through, about 5 minutes. Keep warm.

For the sauce, heat the oil in a non-stick saucepan over medium-high heat. Add the onion, ginger, and garlic and cook for 4 minutes. Add the cumin seeds and cook for 10 seconds, stirring constantly. Add the tomato paste and cook for about 10 seconds. Stir in the green chili, garam masala, fenugreek leaves, turmeric, and salt. Reduce the heat to medium and cook for 2 or 3 minutes.

Stir in the crushed tomatoes, spinach, and water, and bring the sauce to a boil. Reduce the heat to a simmer, cover with a lid, and cook for 10 minutes. Add the meatballs to the sauce and cook for 1 minute on low heat, or until the meatballs are heated through. Turn the heat off and let sit for 5 minutes before serving.

NOTE For a vegetarian dish, replace the meatballs with 2 lb of pan-fried paneer chunks or extra-firm tofu.

SUGGESTED WINE Serve this dish with a medium-bodied red such as the Mission Hill Family Estate Five Vineyards Pinot Noir.

SERVES 4

This recipe was inspired by steak with peppercorn sauce. I like New York steak, but you can use any cut. Fennel seed is called **saunf** *in Punjabi. The seeds are pale green, strongly aromatic, and usually chewed as a breath freshener after a meal.*

new york steak with fennel seeds

2 tsp whole fennel seeds
1 tsp ground cumin
1 tsp ground coriander
¼ tsp salt
¼ tsp pepper
4 New York steaks, 8 oz each

Preheat the barbecue to medium. Place the fennel seeds, cumin, coriander, salt, and pepper in a bowl and mix well. Rub the mixture on both sides of each steak.

Grill the steaks until done to your preference, about 5 to 7 minutes on each side for rare.

Serve the steak with Ginger Potatoes (page 104). Punjabi Asparagus (page 118) makes a nice side dish.

SUGGESTED WINE Shiraz or Cabernet Sauvignon

SERVES 4

In my village, buffalo and cows were not killed for meat; they were respected and taken care of for various sociological and religious reasons. Once I was in Canada I tried all kinds of meat, including buffalo. The complex blend of spices in this dish makes it one of my favourites. It also freezes well.

buffalo masala

1 cup yogurt
½ cup chickpea flour
3 cups water
2 Tbsp grapeseed oil
2 Tbsp chopped garlic
2 Tbsp grated ginger
1 red onion, thinly sliced
1 lb buffalo stewing meat
2 Tbsp Garam Masala (page 12)
1 Tbsp Chana Masala (page 14)
1 tsp ground turmeric
2 cups chopped tomatoes
1 cup store-bought spaghetti sauce
1 tsp salt

Place the yogurt, chickpea flour, and water in a large bowl, and whisk until the flour is completely incorporated and the mixture is smooth. Set aside.

Combine the oil, garlic, ginger, and onion in a non-stick skillet over medium-high heat and cook for 3 minutes. Add the meat, garam masala, chana masala, and turmeric. Stir and cook for 3 minutes.

Add the yogurt mixture, along with the tomatoes, spaghetti sauce, and salt. Cook over medium-low heat until the meat is tender, about 15 minutes, stirring occasionally. Serve on brown rice or with plain rotis (see page 20).

NOTE For additional flavour, I sometimes add 2 green chilies finely chopped, 1 Tbsp fenugreek leaves, and 1 tsp Spanish paprika along with the rest of the spices.

SERVES 4

Buffalo meat is often available in organic and whole food markets. It is usually low in fat. The spices make these burgers aromatic and flavourful.

lean buffalo burgers

- 1 lb lean ground buffalo
- 1 free-range egg
- 1 red onion, finely chopped
- 1 tsp fennel seeds
- 1 tsp Spanish paprika
- 1 tsp fenugreek leaves
- 1 tsp Garam Masala (page 12)
- ½ tsp salt
- 2 Tbsp grapeseed oil

Preheat the barbecue to medium. Combine all the ingredients in a large bowl and gently mix until the spices are evenly distributed. Form into 4 patties.

Place the burgers on the barbecue, and cook until the meat is browned; flip and cook the other side until the burgers are cooked through. Serve on a whole wheat bun with vegetables and condiments of your choice.

SERVES 4

drinks and desserts

We drank this warm tea twice a day every day when I was growing up, once in the morning and once in the evening. It was also served when we had visitors—in fact, it was considered rude if chai was not offered to guests. As much as I love Indian food, I am not crazy about everything in the house smelling like curry, and the best way to get rid of the smell is to make a pot of chai at the end of the meal. It is also very good for the digestive system.

everyday chai

- 4 cups water
- 1-inch piece cinnamon
- 2 cloves
- 2 green cardamom pods
- 1 brown cardamom pod
- 1 tsp grated ginger
- sugar to taste
- 2 Tbsp black tea of your choice (or 1 teabag)
- ¾ cup milk

Mix all the ingredients except the milk in a saucepan. Bring to a boil, then lower the heat and simmer for 10 minutes. Add the milk and bring it to a boil again. Strain the tea and enjoy!

NOTE I most often enjoy this as a herbal drink: just omit the sugar, black tea, and milk.

SERVES 4

I find this is the best remedy at the first sign of a cold or flu. Whenever my dear friend Indira is not feeling well, she tells me this tea is the only thing that helps "cleanse her system."

ginger tea with lemon

1 Tbsp grated ginger
1 tsp grated lemon rind
1 cup boiling water

Place the ginger and lemon in a strainer in a mug and pour the hot water over top. Let it steep for 2 minutes. Remove the strainer and enjoy!

NOTE For a sweet touch, add 1 tsp honey.

SERVES 1

Sometimes I forget to make dessert when I cook for guests. This one is very quick and can be made from ingredients on hand in the freezer and pantry. Everyone loves this little sweet and sour cold dessert at the end of a delicious spicy meal.

guilt-free fruit shake

- 1 cup canned peaches
- ½ cup canned pineapple tidbits
- 1 cup ice cubes
- 2 cups plain frozen yogurt
- 1 Tbsp lemon juice

Place the peaches, pineapple, and ice cubes in a blender and mix until the fruit is finely puréed. Add the yogurt and lemon juice and blend until the yogurt is evenly mixed in. Enjoy!

SERVES 2

I had the honour of cooking for a fund-raising event for children with AIDS in Africa. I was preparing healthy Indian meals, and my team decided to make a quick snack as well. I wanted it to be a no-mess, healthy finger food and decided on these cookies. They received an overwhelmingly positive response, and I was told that no one would guess these cookies were made with lentils unless they actually saw the recipe.

bal's healthy cookies

- ¾ cup margarine
- ¾ cup brown sugar
- 1 egg
- 1 cup mixed lentils, cooked, drained well, and puréed
- 2 tsp vanilla
- 2 cups quick rolled oats
- 1½ cups whole wheat flour
- 1 tsp baking soda
- ½ tsp salt
- ½ cup chocolate chips
- 1 cup slivered almonds
- ¼ cup pumpkin seeds

Preheat the oven to 375°F. Grease a cookie sheet.

Cream the margarine and sugar together. Add the egg and mix well. Stir in the lentil purée and vanilla. Add the rest of the ingredients and mix everything well.

Drop by spoonfuls on the baking sheet and flatten with a fork. Bake for 13 to 18 minutes. Cool on a rack.

NOTE For those with egg allergies, ground flaxseed is a good substitute. Place ¼ cup of water and 2 Tbsp ground flaxseed in a bowl. Mix well and let it sit for 15 minutes. A glue-like mixture forms, which works as a binding agent and replaces the egg.

MAKES 10–12 COOKIES

My mother's rice pudding was famous in the village. She made it once or twice a year. After milking the bison, she put the milk straight into a large pot on the barbecue pit. She added white rice and let it cook on very low heat for hours, stirring it occasionally. The non-pasteurized milk would thicken to a rich creamy consistency. In this recipe, I use wholesome brown rice, and, instead of sugar, organic brown rice syrup, which is available in health food stores. This is a quick, tasty, and guilt-free dessert.

bal's rice pudding

- 4 cups 2% milk
- 2 cups cooked brown rice
- ¼ cup slivered almonds
- ¼ cup raisins
- ¼ cup organic brown rice syrup
- 3 green cardamom pods
- 2 cloves

Put all the ingredients in a large pot and bring to a boil. Reduce the heat to low and simmer until the mixture thickens, about 15 minutes, stirring occasionally. Chill before serving.

NOTE I always top this with seasonal fruit, such as mango, strawberry, or papaya.

SERVES 4

I made this recipe for the first time in a cooking class. We did not have dessert on the menu, and I knew some people would be disappointed. I had bought some low-fat frozen yogurt to eat after the class, but I figured I had enough time to gather ingredients for something flavourful. That day I was making mango chutney, so there were plenty of mangoes and fresh lemons, and I asked the owner of the shop where I was teaching if there was any mango drink available at the store. This was the result. The class absolutely raved about this dessert.

mango sherbet

- 2 cups mango juice
- 1 cup ripe mango chunks
- 1 banana
- 2 cups plain frozen yogurt
- 1 Tbsp lemon juice
- 12 thin slices ripe mango (for garnish)

Put the mango juice, mango chunks, and banana in a food processor and process until the mango chunks are chopped. Add the frozen yogurt and lemon juice, and process on low speed until well combined.

Transfer the mixture to a large glass bowl or baking dish, cover, and place in the freezer for 2 hours. (If you have an ice cream maker, process until the mixture is thickened.) Spoon into bowls and arrange 3 slices of mango on each serving.

SERVES 4

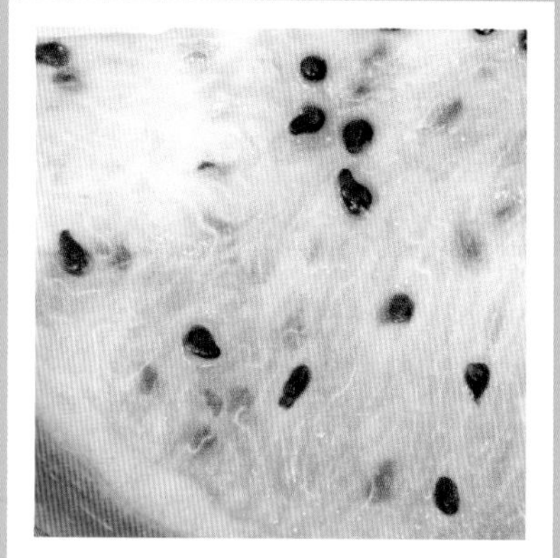

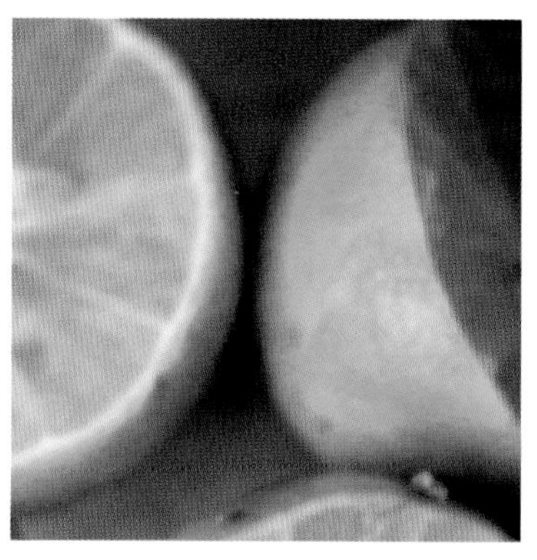

INDEX

Cc

Dd

Ee

Tt

Vv

Ww

Yy

Zz

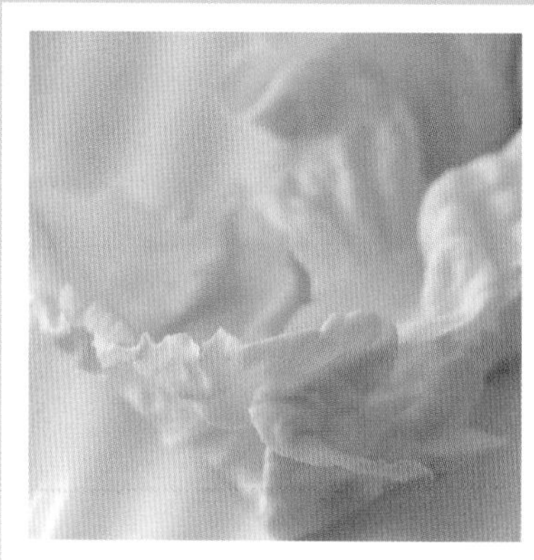

CONVERSION TABLES

Volume	
¼ tsp	1 mL
½ tsp	2 mL
1 tsp	5 mL
½ Tbsp	7.5 mL
2 tsp	10 mL
1 Tbsp	15 mL
2 Tbsp	30 mL
¼ cup	60 mL
⅓ cup	80 mL
½ cup	125 mL
⅔ cup	160 mL
¾ cup	185 mL
1 cup	250 mL
1¼ cups	310 mL
1½ cups	375 mL
2 cups	500 mL
3 cups	750 mL
4 cups	1 L
5 cups	1.25 L
6 cups	1.5 L

Cans	
14 oz can	398 mL

Weight	
6 oz	175 g
½ lb	250 g
1 lb	500 g
1½ lb	750 g
2 lb	1 kg

Temperature	
300°F	150°C
325°F	160°C
350°F	180°C
375°F	190°C
400°F	200°C
425°F	220°C
450°F	230°C
485°F	250°C

Length	
¼ inch	6 mm
½ inch	1 cm
1 inch	2.5 cm
1½ inches	4 cm
2 inches	5 cm
3 inches	8 cm
4 inches	10 cm
5 inches	12 cm
7 inches	18 cm
9 inches	23 cm
20 inches	50 cm

THANKS

Thanks to Brad, Anoop, Aaron, Donna, George, and Russ Arneson, and Sushil Kaur.

We would like to acknowledge Denby and Oneida for providing the props for the photo shoots, Capers Whole Foods for donating the ingredients, Mission Hill Winery and Eden West Gourmet Kitchen for the wine pairing information, and Mourad from RightFoot.ca.